CONOR McPHERSON

Conor McPherson was born in Dublin in 1971 and attended University College Dublin where he began to write and direct. Original stage plays include *Rum & Vodka*, *The Good Thief*, *This Lime Tree Bower*, *St Nicholas*, *The Weir* (Olivier, Evening Standard and Critics Circle Awards), *Dublin Carol*, *Port Authority*, *Shining City* (Tony Award-nominated), *The Seafarer* (Tony, Olivier and Evening Standard Award nominations), *The Veil* and *The Night Alive* (New York Drama Critics' Circle Award for Best Play). His 2020 adaptation of Chekhov's *Uncle Vanya* won the South Bank Show Sky Arts Theatre Award and was broadcast by BBC TV and PBS in the United States.

His collaboration with Bob Dylan, *Girl from the North Country*, opened at The Old Vic, London, before transferring to the West End (winning two Olivier Awards) and Broadway, where it was nominated for seven Tony Awards, including Best Musical, Best Director, Best Book of a Musical, and won the Tony for Best Orchestrations.

Awards for his screenwriting include four Best Screenplay Awards from the Irish Film and Television Academy; Spanish Screenwriters' Circle Best Screenplay Award; the CICAE award for Best Film from the Berlin Film Festival; the Jury Prize from the San Sebastián Film Festival; and the Méliès d'argent award for Best European Film.

BOB DYLAN

Bob Dylan is one of the world's most influential and groundbreaking artists. Since first bursting into the public's consciousness via New York City's Greenwich Village folk music scene in the 1960s, Bob Dylan has sold more than 125 million records and amassed a singular body of work that includes some of the greatest and most popular songs the world has ever known. He continues to traverse the globe, performing more than eighty-five concerts annually.

Dylan's work as an author and visual artist has further burnished his popularity and acclaim: a worldwide best-selling memoir, *Chronicles Vol. 1*, spent nineteen weeks on the *New York Times* Best-Seller list in 2004, and several major exhibitions of his artwork have been shown at some of the world's most prestigious museums and galleries. Bob Dylan's contributions to our culture have been recognised with numerous honours and accolades.

In 2012, Dylan was awarded America's highest civilian honour, the Presidential Medal of Freedom, by President Barack Obama. In December 2016, he was awarded the Nobel Prize for Literature by the Swedish Academy 'for having created new poetic expressions within the great American song tradition.'

Conor McPherson

GIRL FROM THE NORTH COUNTRY

Music and Lyrics by
Bob Dylan

NICK HERN BOOKS
London
www.nickhernbooks.co.uk

A Nick Hern Book

Girl from the North Country first published in 2017 by Nick Hern Books Limited, The Glasshouse, 49a Goldhawk Road, London W12 8QP

Reprinted in this revised edition 2022

Introduction copyright © 2017 Conor McPherson
Afterword copyright © 2022 Conor McPherson
The play *Girl from the North Country* copyright © 2017, 2022 Conor McPherson

Copyright information for the individual songs may be found at the back of the book

Conor McPherson has asserted his moral right to be identified as the author of this work

Cover image: © Runaway Entertainment

Designed and typeset by Nick Hern Books, London
Printed in the UK by Mimeo Ltd, Huntingdon, Cambridgeshire PE29 6XX

A CIP catalogue record for this book is available from the British Library

ISBN   978 1 83904 118 1

Introduction

Maybe five years ago I was asked if I might consider writing a play to feature Bob Dylan's songs. I initially didn't feel this was something I could do and I had cast it out of my mind when, one day, walking along, I saw a vision of a guesthouse in Minnesota in the 1930s.

I had been in Minnesota twice in the years leading up to this – both times in the dead of winter. The friendliness of the people, the dry frozen wind, the vast distance from home, these things had stayed with me. And I saw a way Mr Dylan's songs might make sense in a play.

I was invited to write down the idea I had seen and send it to Bob Dylan. A few days later I heard back that Mr Dylan liked the idea and was happy for me to proceed. Just like that.

And then I received forty albums in the post, covering Mr Dylan's career. While I owned Dylan albums already, like *Desire* and *Blood on the Tracks*, and loved many of his songs (often without knowing he'd written them) performed by hundreds of artists from The Byrds to Fairport Convention, I had no idea of the real search he had been on his whole life.

It strikes me that many of Mr Dylan's songs can be sung at any time, by anyone in any situation, and still make sense and resonate with that particular place and person and time. When you realise this you can no longer have any doubt you are in the presence of a truly great, unique artist.

Working on our production of *Girl from the North Country*, sometimes I would wake in the night with a Bob Dylan song going round in my head. The next day I would come into rehearsals and we'd learn the song and put it in the show. Did it fit? Did it matter? It always fit somehow.

Many books have been written in an attempt to explore this universal power. Even though Mr Dylan will say he's often not sure what his songs mean, he always sings them like he means them. Because he does mean them. Whatever they mean.

Every time I hear these songs I see a picture like I'm watching a movie. Sometimes it's the same, sometimes it's different, but you always see something.

Like Philip Larkin, like James Joyce, Mr Dylan has the rare power of literary compression. Images and conceits are held in unstable relations, forcing an atomic reaction of some kind, creating a new inner world.

But let's talk about his musicality. Spending time with his music has taught me a few things: Firstly, writing something that sounds original is rare, but writing something that sounds original *and* simple at the same time is the mark of genius. Anyone can keep making things more complicated, but to keep a song simple, like it somehow always existed and would have surely been written by someone, someday… try writing that one.

Secondly, Mr Dylan always goes through the right musical door. Listening to a Bob Dylan song is like being in a room you've never been in before. It's full of characters and images and tons of musical atmosphere. But then Bob changes the chords, moving through a bridge or a chorus, and a door opens up in that room, so you go through that door into another room – but it's always the *right* door.

Thirdly, Mr Dylan sings about God a lot. Sometimes God appears as an impossible reflection of yourself. Sometimes as someone you could never know. But however God appears, however Mr Dylan begs for mercy, you understand that cry.

Anyway, I write this on the eve of moving from the rehearsal room to the theatre. Whatever happens next I have no idea. All I can say with any certainty is that having had Mr Dylan's trust to create a piece of work using his songs has been one of the great artistic privileges of my life.

Conor McPherson
London, June 2017

Girl from the North Country premiered at The Old Vic, London, on 8 July 2017, with the following cast (in alphabetical order) and creative team:

MARIANNE LAINE	Sheila Atim
DR WALKER	Ron Cook
MRS BURKE	Bronagh Gallagher
ELIZABETH LAINE	Shirley Henderson
NICK LAINE	Ciarán Hinds
KATHERINE DRAPER	Claudia Jolly
JOE SCOTT	Arinzé Kene
MRS NEILSEN	Debbie Kurup
ENSEMBLE	Kirsty Malpass
MR PERRY	Jim Norton
ENSEMBLE	Tom Peters
ENSEMBLE	Karl Queensborough
GENE LAINE	Sam Reid
REVEREND MARLOWE	Michael Shaeffer
ELIAS BURKE	Jack Shalloo
MR BURKE	Stanley Townsend

Director	Conor McPherson
Music and Lyrics	Bob Dylan
Designer	Rae Smith
Orchestrator, Arranger and Musical Supervisor	Simon Hale
Lighting Designer	Mark Henderson
Sound Designer	Simon Baker
Musical Director	Alan Berry
Movement Director	Lucy Hind
Casting Director	Jessica Ronane CDG

The production transferred to the Noël Coward Theatre, London, on 29 December 2017, with the following changes to the cast:

ENSEMBLE	Hannah Azuonye
ENSEMBLE	Ross Dawes
ENSEMBLE	Mary Doherty
MR BURKE	David Ganly
DR WALKER	Adam James

MR PERRY	Karl Johnson
ENSEMBLE	Emmanuel Kojo
REVEREND MARLOWE	Finbar Lynch

The production received its North American premiere at the Belasco Theatre, New York City, on 7 February 2020, with the following cast:

ELIAS BURKE	Todd Almond
MRS NEILSEN	Jeannette Bayardelle
SWING	Jennifer Blood
SWING	Law Terrell Dunford
ENSEMBLE	Matthew Harris
KATHERINE DRAPER	Caitlin Houlahan
DR WALKER	Robert Joy
MR BURKE	Marc Kudisch
MRS BURKE	Luba Mason
SWING	Ben Mayne
REVEREND MARLOWE	Matt McGrath
MR PERRY	Tom Nelis
GENE LAINE	Colton Ryan
NICK LAINE	Jay O. Sanders
ENSEMBLE	John Schiappa
JOE SCOTT	Austin Scott
MARIANNE LAINE	Kimber Sprawl
ENSEMBLE	Rachel Stern
SWING	Chiara Trentalange
SWING	Bob Walton
ELIZABETH LAINE	Mare Winningham

The 2022–23 tour of Ireland and the UK premiered at the Olympia Theatre, Dublin, on 25 June 2022, with the following cast:

MRS NEILSEN	Keisha Amponsa Banson
ELIAS BURKE	Ross Carswell
NICK LAINE	Colin Connor
ENSEMBLE	Frankie Hart
JOE SCOTT	Joshua C. Jackson
REVEREND MARLOWE	Eli James

MARIANNE LAINE	Justina Kehinde
MR PERRY	Teddy Kempner
ENSEMBLE	Graham Kent
ENSEMBLE	Owen Lloyd
ENSEMBLE	Nichola MacEvilly
DR WALKER	Chris McHallem
ELIZABETH LAINE	Frances McNamee
GENE LAINE	Gregor Milne
KATHERINE DRAPER	Eve Norris
ENSEMBLE	Daniel Reid-Walters
MR BURKE	James Staddon
ENSEMBLE	Neil Stewart
MRS BURKE	Rebecca Thornhill

For Fionnuala and Sumati

Characters

NICK LAINE, *early fifties, proprietor*
ELIZABETH LAINE, *early fifties, his wife*
MARIANNE LAINE, *nineteen, their daughter*
GENE LAINE, *twenty, their son*
MRS NEILSEN, *early forties, a widow*
MR BURKE, *fifties, erstwhile factory owner*
MRS BURKE, *fifties, his wife*
ELIAS BURKE, *thirty, their son*
JOE SCOTT, *late twenties, a boxer*
REVEREND MARLOWE, *fifties, a Bible salesman*
MR PERRY, *early sixties, a shoe-mender*
DR WALKER, *middle-aged, a physician*
KATHERINE (KATE) DRAPER, *Gene's ex-girlfriend*

Setting

A fair-sized family house, which is now serving as a guesthouse in Duluth, Minnesota. Winter, 1934.

Note on Lyrics

An ellipsis (…) on its own line indicates an omitted verse or chorus from within the original song.

ACT ONE

Sign On The Window

ALL.

Sign on the window says 'Lonely'
Sign on the door said 'No Company Allowed'
Sign on the street says 'Y' Don't Own Me'
Sign on the porch says 'Three's A Crowd'
Sign on the porch says 'Three's A Crowd'

…

Looks like a-nothing but rain…
Sure gonna be wet tonight on Main Street…
Hope that it don't sleet.

The band take the music down for a few bars while DR
WALKER *approaches the microphone:*

DR WALKER. Tonight's story begins and ends at a guesthouse
in Duluth, Minnesota, in the winter of 1934. Back here –
some of the guests we'll meet along the way.

*The rising light reveals two figures in the dining room where
there's a table for eating at, some easy chairs near a stove, a
dresser, a piano.* ELIZABETH, *fifties, has early-onset
dementia. Her husband,* NICK, *is the same age as*
ELIZABETH *but an agitated energy makes him seem
younger somehow. He puts on an apron and starts working,
setting the table for their guests.*

This is Nick Laine. That's his wife there, Elizabeth. Nick
inherited this house from his granddaddy, but he never had no
head for business. First he lost the stables and stud, then all
the stocks. Managed to remortgage the house long enough for
Elizabeth to turn it into decent boarding rooms.

NICK *takes a revolver from his pocket and examines it.*
ELIZABETH *shoves him. He gives her a dirty look and puts
the gun away.*

But she hasn't been so good lately. Nick's tryna take care of everything. Trying real hard. Like a man tryna run through a wall tries real hard.

My name is George Arthur Walker. I'm a doctor. Least I was. Back when this was our world. I healed some bodies in pain. But as we know pain comes in all kinds. Physical, spiritual. Indescribable.

I'll come in the story later, but right now, all you need to know is Nick's made some stew for his family, for the guests. Keep everybody alive another day.

NICK *spoons stew in a bowl to cool for* ELIZABETH. *The song finishes out...*

NICK. Elizabeth. (*Pause.*) Elizabeth.

She ignores him.

Elizabeth. Sit down, I'll give you something to eat.

ELIZABETH*'s expression suggests her absence, her presence. She looks at him but otherwise ignores his requests. She goes, bends down under a chair and retrieves a little box. She turns away, hiding it from* NICK. *She opens it, counts through some dollars in there, and closes it again quickly.*

Sit down. Come on. Supper.

Exasperated, he puts her meal down on the table and comes to her, guiding her towards the easy chair near the stove. She resists. This becomes a silent battle of wills as they wrestle. She is surprisingly strong. NICK *gives up, angrily walking away and tossing a plate across the table. She remains standing.*

Alright. Well. Alright.

ELIZABETH. I can hear it.

NICK. What.

ELIZABETH. The girl down the hole.

NICK *looks at her.*

NICK. What?

ELIZABETH. Girl down the hole.

NICK *is startled by someone coming through the kitchen.*

NICK. Hello?

NICK *sees* GENE *in the kitchen.*

Oh.

GENE. Yeah, 'Oh...'

NICK. What are you doing scratching around like that?

GENE. What? I'm hungry!

NICK. You know what time it is? You're only coming in?

GENE. I was working late.

NICK. Working my ass.

GENE. I was working!

NICK. You were drinking.

GENE. You have to drink if you want to sit at the bar.

NICK. Who works in a bar?! You can't write in your room?

GENE. No I can't write in my room.

NICK. Why?

GENE. It's too stultifying.

NICK. Well excuse me! I saw you got a letter. Huh?

GENE. Yeah.

NICK. New York postmark.

GENE. It was nothing.

NICK. Yeah?

GENE. Yeah, nothing, you know.

NICK. You should let me read, you know, some of your short stories, sometime.

GENE. Yeah?

NICK. Hey I been around.

GENE. Yeah.

NICK. Yeah. I've lived. You can't see it 'cause as far as you're concerned I'm just the old dumb-bell round here. I could read 'em. Tell ya where you might need a little... you know. A little life. A little real life. Maybe we could turn some a those rejection slips into paychecks, huh?

GENE. Now I know you're desperate.

NICK. Desperate? Well...

GENE. Two minutes ago it wasn't even work, now you wanna do it for me?

NICK. Hey don't ambush me with my own double standards. You don't even know what work is. Get a job, you'll know all about it. What it does to you.

GENE. Get a job where?

NICK (*to himself*). Scribbling in a book isn't work.

GENE. Get a job where?

NICK. Hm?

GENE. Get a job where?

NICK. What are you asking me for? The Twin Cities! I don't know! You and your sister are too damn spoiled. You wanna give me some help here?

GENE. What do you want?

NICK. Set the table. Feed your mother.

GENE. She doesn't want me feeding her!

NICK. You do it too fast. Let her chew, for Christ's sake! You let it all go down her chin, of course she doesn't like it.

GENE. She doesn't like me doing it, she doesn't like me... [doing it.]

NICK. It's because you don't pay attention.

NICK *is checking his watch.*

GENE. What's up your nose all of a sudden?

NICK. What?

GENE. Why you so on edge?

NICK. I'm not on edge.

GENE. No, huh?

> MRS NEILSEN, *a woman in her forties, comes into focus.*
> *She wears a skirt with pockets in it. When she has her hands*
> *in her pockets she takes on a kind of lounging adolescent*
> *rebelliousness. She sings.*

Went To See The Gypsy

MRS NEILSEN.
> Went to see the gypsy
> Stayin' in a big hotel
> He smiled when he saw me coming
> And he said, 'Well, well, well'
> His room was dark and crowded
> Lights were low and dim
> 'How are you?' he said to me
> I said it back to him
>
> I went down to the lobby
> To make a small call out
> A pretty dancing girl was there
> And she began to shout
> 'Go on back to see the gypsy
> He can move you from the rear
> Drive you from your fear
> Bring you through the mirror
> He did it in Las Vegas
> And he can do it here'
> Outside the lights were shining
> On the river of tears
> I watched them from the distance
> With music in my ears

NICK. Mrs Neilsen.

MRS NEILSEN. Mr Laine. How are you all this evening?

NICK. All fine, thank you.

MRS NEILSEN. Gene.

GENE. Mrs Neilsen.

NICK. We have chicken stew if you're hungry.

MRS NEILSEN. It smells very good.

> GENE *slips away.* NICK *tries to feed a reluctant* ELIZABETH.

NICK. I fixed that window was banging in your room.

MRS NEILSEN. I saw that, thank you. Wind's picking up.

NICK. There's a storm due.

MRS NEILSEN. It's making it rattle a little.

NICK. Oh?

> MRS NEILSEN *comes to* NICK.

MRS NEILSEN. You want to come and fix it tonight?

NICK. I don't know. I'm...

MRS NEILSEN. Fix my window.

> MRS NEILSEN *tries to touch him playfully.*

NICK (*whispers*). Not in front of Elizabeth, alright?

MRS NEILSEN. She's not watching.

> ELIZABETH *looks at* NICK.

NICK (*doubtfully*). Yeah...

> MRS NEILSEN *holds her newspaper where* NICK *can see it.*

MRS NEILSEN. You see this one?

> NICK *glances at it. Looks at her.*

NICK. You could afford that?

MRS NEILSEN. Depends, I guess. But look at it. It's got a real restaurant. Twenty-two rooms. We could whip it into shape.

NICK. Twenty-two rooms, huh?

MRS NEILSEN. We could handle it. With your experience and my charisma.

NICK. Yeah. Up in Bismark...

MRS NEILSEN. You don't like Bismark?

NICK. Three guys I knew from Bismark always cheated at cards.

MRS NEILSEN (*whipping newspaper away*). Oh right, what was I thinking?

NICK. Don't get sore! It's a great idea. I just wish I could think straight.

MRS NEILSEN. What's to think about? You got some other plan?

NICK. Your money comes through, I'll be full a plans.

MRS NEILSEN. It'll come through. Don't be so pessimistic.

NICK. Yeah, I know. Just... Bismark...

She sees him checking his watch.

MRS NEILSEN. What are you up to?

NICK. I'm not up to nothing.

MRS NEILSEN. Why do you keep looking at your watch?

NICK. Do I? Just wondering. Where Marianne is.

MRS NEILSEN. She's a grown woman.

NICK. She has a baby inside her! Can't be traipsing up and down the streets! In the cold. Mr Perry's calling by, and...

MRS NEILSEN. The shoe-mender?

NICK. Mm-hm.

MRS NEILSEN. For what?

NICK. He's a good man.

MRS NEILSEN. So?

NICK (*as though* MRS NEILSEN *is missing something very obvious*). So...

MRS NEILSEN. He must be seventy if he's a day!

NICK. He's not seventy!

MRS NEILSEN. So what is he? Sixty-nine and three quarters?
The girl is nineteen!

NICK (*shrugs*). She needs a husband.

MRS NEILSEN. What for?

NICK. Take care of her. The father's jumped on a damn lake
boat – probably down in Toledo by now.

MRS NEILSEN. Maybe she doesn't need a husband.

NICK. Oh yeah? Well where's she gonna go?

MRS NEILSEN. Why does she have to go anywhere?

NICK. Because… it's… (*Suddenly changes tack, picking on*
MRS NEILSEN *irritably.*) What do you care? When your
probate comes through, you know what you'll do? You'll just
get back on the train and go back to Minneapolis – and why
shouldn't you?

MRS NEILSEN (*rising to his irritable tone*). Well I can't live in
a boarding house forever, can I? (*Indicates* ELIZABETH.)
With your wife!

NICK. With my what? She was finished with me anyway!

MRS NEILSEN. So *you* say.

NICK. Before she got sick! She told me straight out.

MRS NEILSEN. Yeah…

NICK. And now she's just forgotten! When someone turns round
just says, 'I don't love you anymore', you know what the
shock is? There ain't nothing you can do! That's it! You can't
make 'em love ya. People love dirtbags all over the world…

MRS NEILSEN (*wryly*). Tell me about it.

NICK. Even name the damn children after 'em!

ELIZABETH. Marriage is a sacrament.

NICK. Doesn't mean anyone's gotta love you.

MRS NEILSEN. Well maybe someone does, Nick – you ever thought a that?

She turns away and sits at the table to eat. Segue back to 'Went To See The Gypsy':

MRS NEILSEN.
          I went back to see the gypsy
          It was nearly early dawn
          The gypsy's door was open wide
          But the gypsy was gone
          And that pretty dancing girl
          She could not be found
          So I watched that sun come rising
          From that little Minnesota town
          From that little Minnesota…

          (*Speaing*.) You ain't finished with her, Nick.

NICK (*unconvinced*). Yeah?

MRS NEILSEN. You don't know it?

NICK. I don't know nothing no more.

          GENE *brings in* MR PERRY. MR PERRY *carries a little bunch of winter flowers.*

MR PERRY. Behold! An angel of the Lord appeared to Joseph in a dream!

NICK. Mr Perry!

MR PERRY. Mr Laine.

NICK. Come in, come in.

MR PERRY. Why, thank you.

NICK. You know Mrs Neilsen.

MR PERRY. I've seen you.

MRS NEILSEN. Yes, we've… (*Indicates 'seen each other'*.)

NICK. Mrs Neilsen is a guest here. She… has business here… When her business is done she'll be…

MR PERRY. Well I hope you find Duluth to be as hospitable as we suppose it to be?

MRS NEILSEN. It's a fine, beautiful city.

MR PERRY. Yes, well we like to think so.

NICK. Gene, of course, you know.

MR PERRY *smiles at* GENE.

And Elizabeth.

MR PERRY. Of course. How are you this evening, Mrs Laine?

ELIZABETH *gives him a withering look and turns away.*

NICK And I... Gene, where's Marianne?

GENE. I don't know.

NICK. Will you see if maybe she came in, please?

NICK *clips* GENE *around the ear.*

Will you look in her room? (*To* MR PERRY, *re:* GENE.)
Such a great kid!

GENE *goes.*

Well... There's a stormy night!

MR PERRY. Yes. I swore I'd make it up that hill.

NICK. It's a-blowin'!

ELIZABETH (*drily*). Good one, Popeye...

Strained smiles from MR PERRY *and* MRS NEILSEN.

You take a drink? A glass of beer?

MR PERRY. A glass of milk would be...

NICK. Right!

MRS NEILSEN. I'll get it.

MR PERRY. Not too cold!

NICK. Not too cold!

MRS NEILSEN. You want me to warm it up?

MR PERRY. No – room temperature is fine.

NICK. Room temperature.

MRS NEILSEN. Any particular room?

MR PERRY. This one's good.

MRS NEILSEN. Alright.

She goes to get the milk.

NICK. How's the... How's things in the shoe-mending business? If that's not a personal question.

MR PERRY. Not at all. My store is full of shoes. I'm occupied from daybreak 'til dark. Thank the Lord.

NICK. You're occupied.

MR PERRY. Yes, sir.

NICK. How long has it been since your wife passed?

MR PERRY. Twelve years.

NICK. Twelve years, huh?

MR PERRY. That's right.

NICK. That's uh...

MR PERRY. Yeah, it's a long time I guess.

NICK. Twelve years is a long time. It's a chunk of change.

MR PERRY. Well.

MRS NEILSEN *comes behind* MR PERRY *with the milk, startling him.*

Jesus!

NICK. What are you doing?

MRS NEILSEN. What?! It's room temperature.

MR PERRY. Thank you.

ELIZABETH. You're welcome.

NICK. You know how Marianne came to be our daughter, right?

MR PERRY. I heard something...

NICK. Someone checked out – left a bag on the bed and you know what was in it?

ELIZABETH (*claps her hands three times quickly*). Marianne!

NICK. Marianne! She was only a baby. I mean we tried to find the parents. Seemed the best thing was to let her stay here. Elizabeth took care of her. No one ever came back.

MR PERRY. You're good people.

NICK. I don't know. I guess. Elizabeth always wanted a daughter.

ELIZABETH. He already lost one baby girl.

MR PERRY *smiles at* ELIZABETH, *who looks at* MR PERRY *inscrutably.*

NICK (*desperate for something to say*). Mrs Neilsen is a widow.

MRS NEILSEN *winces at this label, but smiles through it.*

MR PERRY. Oh, I am sorry.

MRS NEILSEN. Thank you.

NICK. Her husband is dead. She was up in St Paul.

MR PERRY. I see.

NICK. Husband died three years ago, she's still waiting on his will to be cleared!

MR PERRY. Oh.

NICK. Charles St Clair, here in Duluth…

MR PERRY. Mm-hm.

NICK. He's doing the paperwork. It'll get cleared out. She's got a favorable rate here and it'll all…

MRS NEILSEN. Yes – thank you, Nick!

MRS NEILSEN *smiles through gritted teeth.*

MR PERRY. Your husband have ties here?

MRS NEILSEN. He was in the railroad business. He had shares in the line.

MR PERRY (*impressed*). Right…

NICK. He's dead.

MRS NEILSEN. They have all the right paperwork now. It won't take long. And then I'll…

MR PERRY. You'll buy a house here in Duluth.

MRS NEILSEN No. I'll…

NICK. She'll spread her wings.

ELIZABETH. Are those flowers for me?

MR PERRY looks at the flowers. NICK looks, aghast, at
ELIZABETH.

NICK. Now, Elizabeth…

ELIZABETH. They're pretty.

MR PERRY. Well, they're for, eh… why, well, yes, they're…
They're for you.

She doesn't take them.

ELIZABETH. Can you remember? When you asked me and asked me and asked me to come with you to the Cook County Fair?

MR PERRY smiles, unsure what to say.

NICK. Well now, Elizabeth, I'm sure that wasn't Mr Perry…

ELIZABETH. Can you remember? The lights? And how dark it was afterwards walking home together and what you said to me? Begging me to touch it?

NICK. Elizabeth, now, please!

ELIZABETH. 'For the love of mercy, please just hold it, Elizabeth,' you said.

MR PERRY. Well now I…

ELIZABETH. 'Just hold it. Just touch it. I'm begging you.' Do you remember?

NICK. For Christ's sake, Elizabeth… I'm sorry, Mr Perry.

ELIZABETH. And I said, 'Why, it's just like a tiny Vienna sausage!'

NICK. I'm so sorry.

ELIZABETH. How I cried afterwards – I was only a girl. Goodnight.

NICK. Goodnight, Elizabeth.

ELIZABETH *slyly takes a knife from the table.* NICK *spots this, lunging at her before she can get to* MR PERRY. MRS NEILSEN *and* NICK *wrestle the knife from* ELIZABETH *as* MARIANNE *comes in. She is nineteen and the only black member of her white family.*

NICK. Marianne! You're... Look who's here.

MR PERRY. Good evening, Marianne.

MARIANNE. Mr Perry.

NICK. Well I'm... (*Stretches, yawns.*) We should really start getting Elizabeth to bed. Mrs Neilsen, would you mind? I hate to impinge...

MRS NEILSEN (*pointedly to* NICK). Not at all. Come on, Elizabeth, I'll brush your teeth.

ELIZABETH. And sing?

MRS NEILSEN. Sure, alright then.

NICK. Goodnight, honey.

MR PERRY. Goodnight, Elizabeth.

ELIZABETH. Goodnight, Mr Peepee.

MRS NEILSEN *takes* ELIZABETH *out.*

NICK. Marianne, you'll...

He nods repeatedly at MARIANNE *to make her stay.*

MARIANNE (*to* MR PERRY). Would you like something to eat?

MR PERRY. No I'm fine.

NICK. I'll just... I gotta fix the commode.

MARIANNE. He broke it.

NICK goes, leaving MARIANNE *and* MR PERRY *alone.*
MR PERRY *still holds his flowers and his milk.*

MARIANNE *gets herself some supper.*

MARIANNE (*indicating food*). Are you sure?

MR PERRY. Yes, thank you. Well, this is nice. (*As she eats.*) Is it good?

MARIANNE. My pa can't cook for shit.

MR PERRY. I can cook.

MARIANNE. I'll bet.

MR PERRY. You are finished your schooling now I believe.

MARIANNE. Yes, sir.

MR PERRY. Now, Marianne. I'm going to be frank with you. Your father has spoken with me and I am aware of your... I am aware of your condition. My house is warm, it's centrally located. My habits are regular. I will wed you, Marianne, and parent the child.

MARIANNE. Mr Perry, your offer is very kind but...

MR PERRY (*talks over her*). I'm a deal older than you. I may not look it, but it's true. I won't be round for ever. Time comes, you'll have the whole place. Child'll be reared, and you'll be free – and still a relatively young woman. Now there's a deal and if I ever heard better it's gone from my mind.

MARIANNE. Mr Perry, I couldn't.

MR PERRY. It's a lot to take in. I get it. I really do. But you sleep on it.

MARIANNE. Mr Perry, I...

She goes to speak again but he silences her.

MR PERRY. You sleep on it! Inspiration comes in dreams!

He leaves. MARIANNE *sings.*

Tight Connection To My Heart (Has Anyone Seen My Love)

MARIANNE.

> Well, I had to move fast
> And I couldn't with you around my neck
> I said I'd send for you and I did
> What did you expect?
> My hands are sweating
> And we haven't even started yet
> I'll go along with the charade
> Until I can think my way out
> I know it was all a big joke
> Whatever it was about
> Someday maybe
> I'll remember to forget
>
> I'm gonna get my coat
> I feel the breath of a storm
> There's something I've got to do tonight
> You go inside and stay warm
>
> Has anybody seen my love
> Has anybody seen my love
> Has anybody seen my love
> I don't know
> Has anybody seen my love?
>
> You want to talk to me
> Go ahead and talk
> Whatever you got to say to me
> Won't come as any shock
> I must be guilty of something
> You just whisper it into my ear
> Madame Butterfly
> She lulled me to sleep
> In a town without pity
> Where the water runs deep
> She said, 'Be easy, baby
> There ain't nothin' worth stealin' in here'
>
> You're the one I've been looking for
> You're the one that's got the key
> But I can't figure out whether I'm too good for you
> Or you're too good for me

Has anybody seen my love
Has anybody seen my love
Has anybody seen my love
I don't know
Has anybody seen my love?

As the music ends, there is a flash of lightning and a thunderclap. Some hours have passed. It's the middle of the night. Rain pours down outside and wind blows. NICK is still working, fixing things up in the house.

A middle-aged white man, REVEREND MARLOWE, and a young athletic-looking black man, JOE SCOTT, come through – cold, drenched and hungry-looking.

MARLOWE. Sir, I am the Reverend James Marlowe, this young man is Joseph Scott Esquire. The Spalding has no vacancies. They recommended your fine house.

NICK. Well come in out of the rain and let's see what we can do. Come on.

MARLOWE. Thank you.

SCOTT. Thank you, sir.

NICK. I have a small room in the back, it'll do one of you. Someone can bunk on that settle in here, it makes a decent cot, if you don't mind.

He throws a thin, filthy-looking mattress on the floor.

SCOTT. I'll sleep anywhere. A chair is fine for me, sir.

NICK. No, you can stretch on out there. I'll charge you a half-dollar. And let's say a dollar fifty for the room in back for yourself.

MARLOWE. A dollar fifty?

NICK. That's right. It's normally two dollars. But considering it's three-thirty in the morning I'll give you a discount. And a half a dollar for the settle here.

SCOTT reaches into his pockets, counts coins into NICK's hand. NICK turns to MARLOWE, who hands him two dollars. NICK instantly sticks MARLOWE with all of SCOTT's change.

And there's your change. Now what do you say, you gents have a glass of whiskey?

MARLOWE. Well that would be a godsend.

SCOTT. Thank you, sir.

NICK *goes to pour them a drink.*

NICK. You can hang those wet coats up yonder.

SCOTT. Yes, sir.

NICK. So, no room at the inn over at The Spalding, huh?

MARLOWE. That's correct.

NICK (*dubious*). Mmm.

MARLOWE. The eleven o'clock from St Paul was delayed.

NICK. You boys travelling together?

MARLOWE. No, sir. We are thrown together by circumstance. Decided to walk on up here together.

NICK. You say you're a reverend?

MARLOWE. That is correct, sir.

NICK. You planning to preach the word?

MARLOWE. I don't preach the word, sir. I sell it. A devil pursues me and his name is commerce.

NICK. You're a Bible salesman?

MARLOWE. In its most basic terms, yes.

NICK. You selling much?

MARLOWE. If I sell two Bibles a day, three, I can live.

NICK (*hands MARLOWE a drink*). Mind if you don't go selling 'em in here?

MARLOWE. Beneath your roof the word is free.

MARLOWE *knocks back his drink.*

NICK. That's two bits for the whiskey. You'll find it's the highest quality.

MARLOWE (*coughs as the liquor burns his throat*). As the price suggests.

SCOTT *refuses the drink* NICK *offers him.*

NICK (*taking coins from* MARLOWE). What's the most you ever owed anybody?

MARLOWE. Excuse me?

NICK. What's the most money you ever had to pay back to someone? Twenty thousand dollars?

MARLOWE. Well no, not *that* kind of...

NICK. You try walking round with that kind of money hanging over you, my friend. You try it for a day. See what it's like. You try it for a lifetime. Never ever invest in the fairground business. Those people are...

MARLOWE. Clowns?

NICK. Mm. (*To* SCOTT.) How about you?

SCOTT. Sir?

NICK. What's your business?

SCOTT. I have an appointment here.

NICK. An appointment? Well alright, there's more blankets in the box. Come on, Reverend, I'll show you. Goodnight.

SCOTT. Goodnight, sir.

MARLOWE. Goodnight, Mr Scott.

SCOTT. Goodnight, Reverend.

NICK *takes* MARLOWE *out the back. Alone in the room,* SCOTT *takes a blanket, wraps it round himself. He is sick, shivering. He coughs and goes toward the glass of whiskey Nick has left behind. Suddenly there's a crash out in the kitchen.* SCOTT *turns round, startled.*

GENE (*from off, cries out in pain*). Ahhh!!

SCOTT. Who's there?

GENE (*coming through to the dining room*). What?

SCOTT. Who's there?

GENE (*drunkenly*). Who am *I*?

SCOTT. Are you alright? What you do?

GENE. *I* don't know! Who is that?

SCOTT. Joseph P. Scott, sir.

GENE *drunkenly crowds* SCOTT.

GENE. You asking me who *I* am? Who are you, boy?

SCOTT. Joseph Scott, sir.

GENE. Uh-huh.

SCOTT. Easy, my man.

GENE. What are you doing in here, boy?

SCOTT. Just stayin' the night. The boss man admitted me himself.

GENE. Oh did he, did he, did he? You tryna start something?

SCOTT. No, sir, I just want a night's sleep. I paid for it.

GENE. You think something is funny?

SCOTT. No, sir.

GENE. You sound like you had some schooling?

SCOTT. Yes, sir.

GENE. Where? Harvard?

GENE *drains the untouched glass of whiskey.*

SCOTT. No, sir, Miss Hemming's schoolhouse, sir. Two-nineteen Washington Street in Brainerd.

GENE. You come on and hit me now.

SCOTT. Sir?

GENE. Hit me. I said hit me.

SCOTT. No, sir.

GENE. You get your black ass up outta that bed and you stand up and you hit me now. You get up and you hit me.

GENE *pulls at* SCOTT. SCOTT *stands up wearily.*

Come on.

SCOTT. I ain't gonna hit you.

GENE. It's alright. You can do it.

SCOTT. I ain't gonna do it.

GENE. Now I said you come and you hit me now or I'm gonna take this poker and I'm gonna stick it through your goddamn eye.

SCOTT. And I said I ain't gonna hit you.

GENE. I say you do as you are told, boy, or you give me one good reason why I don't make you do it.

SCOTT. 'Cause if I hit you, I'll likely kill you.

GENE. What you say?

SCOTT. You heard me.

GENE. Well you done it now.

GENE *swings at* SCOTT. SCOTT *easily knocks* GENE *down with a blow, sending him reeling back across the room.* SCOTT *follows, picking* GENE *up off the floor.*

Alright! Alright! Okay! Okay…

SCOTT. You want me to hit you?

GENE. No.

SCOTT. You want me to hit you some more, boy?

GENE. No.

SCOTT. Huh?

GENE. No.

SCOTT. No what?

GENE. No, sir.

SCOTT. No what?

GENE. No I don't want you to hit me anymore.

MARLOWE comes in wearing his waistcoat and shirt.

MARLOWE. Now there's a man looks like he could use a Bible. James Marlowe. Reverend Jim they call me.

GENE. Right.

MARLOWE. You live here?

GENE. I try.

SCOTT. Where's the convenience?

GENE indicates where the bathroom is, SCOTT goes out.

SCOTT. Goddamn, man, what the hell?

MARLOWE. I just saw you stroke a cat out there on your way in through the backyard. Cat rubbed its fur round your legs like he's the only friend you got in the world. And you know what I thought to myself? What are you gonna do when that cat dies? Have you thought about it? Have you considered death?

GENE. What you say? You're a reverend, huh?

MARLOWE. Yes, sir. The word of God, sir, cloth-bound, gold-embossed, extra-fine print for a mere two dollars. Jesus makes his lifetime of light eminently affordable. Big storm's coming, my boy.

Underscore starts for 'Slow Train'.

Here. Europe. Everywhere. You ever wonder what woulda happened if the Jews met the Vikings? Huh? The Vikings! You know what they woulda done to the Jews?

SCOTT comes back. He tosses GENE a handkerchief to clean himself up. GENE dabs at the blood on his face.

A fine young man like you? Something's wrong somewhere when a fine man like you ain't got two damn dollars – dontcha feel it?

Slow Train

MARLOWE.

Sometimes I feel so low-down and disgusted
Can't help but wonder what's happenin' to my companions
Are they lost or are they found
Have they counted the cost it'll take to bring down
All their earthly principles they're gonna have to abandon?
There's a slow, slow train comin' up around the bend

SCOTT.

I had a woman down in Alabama
She was a backwoods girl, but she sure was realistic
She said, 'Boy, without a doubt
Have to quit your mess and straighten out
You could die down here, be just another accident statistic'
There's a slow, slow train comin' up around the bend

...

Well, my baby went to Illinois with some bad-talkin' boy
    she could destroy
A real suicide case, but there was nothin' I could do to stop it
I don't care about economy
I don't care about astronomy
But it sure do bother me to see my loved ones turning into
    puppets
There's a slow, slow train comin' up around the bend

We segue to 'License To Kill':

License To Kill

FEMALE ENSEMBLE.

There's a woman on my block
She just sit there as the night grows still
She say who gonna take away his license to kill?

MRS NEILSEN.

Now, they take him and they teach him and they groom
    him for life

MARIANNE.

And they set him on a path where he's bound to get ill

FEMALE ENSEMBLE.
>Then they bury him with stars
>Sell his body like they do used cars
>
>Now, there's a woman on my block
>She just sit there facin' the hill
>She say who gonna take away his license to kill?
>
>Ya may be a noisemaker, spirit maker,
>heartbreaker, backbreaker,
>Leave no stone unturned.
>May be an actor in a plot
>That might be all that you got
>'Til your error you clearly learned.

They segue back to 'Slow Train':

SCOTT.
>There's a slow, slow train comin' up around the bend
>A slow, slow train comin' up around the bend.
>A slow train comin.

During the last verse, SCOTT *has lain on the mattress on the floor. The light changes, bringing us to morning.*
MARIANNE comes through the kitchen, carrying breakfast things to the table. ELIZABETH *comes in with her.* SCOTT *turns over.* MARIANNE *halts.*

MARIANNE. Would you like some breakfast?

ELIZABETH. Look what's under the Christmas tree.

MARIANNE. I see it.

SCOTT. Yes thank you.

MARIANNE. The guests like oatmeal. You like it?

SCOTT. Yes, ma'am.

MARIANNE. Coffee is on the way.

SCOTT. What's your name?

MARIANNE. Marianne Laine.

SCOTT. Joseph Scott.

He goes to ELIZABETH.

Joseph Scott, ma'am.

ELIZABETH *takes his hand, and won't let go.* MARIANNE *pulls* ELIZABETH *away.*

MARIANNE. This is my mama. She might say something. She mightn't. She's… [not herself.]

MARIANNE *turns on the wireless. A 1930s-style arrangement of 'Tonight I'll Be Staying Here With You' is playing.*

SCOTT. Pleased to meet you, ma'am.

MARIANNE *starts to fold up* SCOTT*'s bedding.*

MARIANNE. You in Duluth for long?

SCOTT *helps* MARIANNE *fold the bedding.*

SCOTT. No. Couple days, then I head down to Chicago.

MARIANNE. Chicago, huh?

SCOTT. You been there?

MARIANNE. No.

SCOTT. Well you should go someday. It's worth seeing.

MARIANNE. I will.

NICK *and* DR WALKER *come into the kitchen from opposite sides.*

DR WALKER. Morning, Nick, how are you?

NICK (*carrying a table and chair*). You tell me, right?

DR WALKER. You're okay.

NICK. Look who it is, Elizabeth. Doc coming by to see you.

ELIZABETH *embraces* DR WALKER.

DR WALKER. Well there's a welcome you don't get every day.

NICK. She can still spot a good 'un. Breakfast?

DR WALKER. No thank you.

NICK. Have a coffee!

DR WALKER. No – just wanted to drop in Elizabeth's prescription.

NICK. I'd a come by to get it, you didn't need to do that. Stay, have a coffee.

DR WALKER. Well alright.

They meet MR *and* MRS BURKE *arriving down for breakfast with their son,* ELIAS.

ELIAS *is in his thirties but has the mental age of a four-year-old child.* MRS BURKE *is a wiry strong woman and her husband is a balding rotund man. She carries an air of determination. He carries one of defeat, but he doesn't know that.*

MR BURKE. Morning, Doc.

DR WALKER. Folks.

MR BURKE. Good morning.

SCOTT. Good morning, sir.

MR BURKE. William Horace Franklyn Francis Burke the second, this is my wife Laura, my son, Elias.

SCOTT. Joe Scott, the first. Pleased to meet you.

MR BURKE. Dr Walker.

SCOTT. Sir.

MRS NEILSEN *comes through and collects a newspaper from* DR WALKER.

MR BURKE (*as she does so*). Mrs Neilsen.

SCOTT. Ma'am.

ELIAS. Mommy, my scarecrow – (*Searching for a word.*) ah, ah, ah, ah… My scarecrow, ah, ah, ah, my scarecrow wears a hat.

ELIZABETH. What the fuck is wrong with him?

NICK *passes through, carrying tools, doing some maintenance work.*

NICK. Marianne, get some coffee for Dr Walker.

MRS NEILSEN. Now, Mr Laine. Did you hear that? Elias's scarecrow wears a hat, no less.

NICK. I did hear that. Yes, and I saw your scarecrow this morning, Elias. He's looking fine and hardy. Those are some nice twigs you stuck in his... in his head.

Breakfast is underway, with MARIANNE *bringing things in and out and everyone helping themselves.*

MR BURKE. Please correct me if I'm wrong. Haven't I seen you fight, sir?

SCOTT. Oh?

MR BURKE. Saw you knock out Frazier Fitch in Hubertsville, May 1928, am I right?

SCOTT. That's right, sir.

MR BURKE. You're quite a talent. I lost a lot of money that night.

MRS BURKE. Now, Francis, that's your own fault.

MR BURKE. I'm paying him a compliment, my dear.

SCOTT. Thank you, sir.

MR BURKE. You been fighting much?

SCOTT. Well not so much.

MARLOWE *comes in, dressed.*

MARLOWE. Good morning, all. Good morning. James Marlowe.

MR BURKE. William Horace Franklyn Francis Burke the second. Call me Frank. My wife, Laura, Elias. Mrs Laine over there, Mrs Neilsen.

MARLOWE. Pleased to meet you.

MR BURKE. And this young man is Jungle Jug Joe Jones. You know who he is?

MARLOWE. Why yes! We've been acquainted since last night.

MR BURKE. So you know – very talented young man.

MARLOWE. Oh? Not that I'm surprised.

MR BURKE. A rising young man of the pugilistic arts. You been fighting much?

ELIZABETH *finds a coin on the floor and puts it in her little box under her chair.*

SCOTT. Oh not so much.

MR BURKE. Well that's a pity. You should.

SCOTT. Well, I wasn't really able to.

MR BURKE. You injured?

SCOTT. No, I...

MR BURKE. 'Cause a talent like that shouldn't go to waste.

MRS BURKE. No talent should.

MARLOWE (*helping himself to coffee*). Well you know, a man can lose his nerve.

MR BURKE. That can happen, too. You travel round so much, you lose your bearings, you lose the hunger.

MARLOWE. You lose the hunger, Mr Scott?

SCOTT. No, I...

MARLOWE. You get hurt?

SCOTT. No.

MARLOWE. It's alright to run away.

MR BURKE. Well I don't mean to pry. I admire you, sir.

SCOTT. No it's alright, I can tell you. I was incarcerated up in the Stillwater penitentiary for three years.

MR BURKE. Oh, well that's...

SCOTT. A convicted con artiste, name of Rudolf St James, claimed he saw me running from a robbery there April 15th 1929, however his testimony was withdrawn in January this year before a court who declared my conviction to be unsound.

MR BURKE. Well congratulations.

MARLOWE. Well Halleluiah.

ELIZABETH. Well, Halleluiah!

MRS BURKE. What an ordeal.

The music on the wireless segues into a 1930s arrangement of 'Dear Landlord'.

SCOTT. Yes, ma'am. For a man who never smoked, to be stuck inside with men who just burned cigarettes all night. That was maybe the worst part somehow. And the shame of course. For my family.

MRS BURKE. It's terrible.

MR BURKE. You must be itching to get back in the game. You get compensation?

SCOTT. No, sir. I been living under a bridge up in St Paul. A newspaper gentleman named Mose McCabe forwarded me a little money, recommended I talk to a man down here named Mr Murphy might invest in a comeback. But now I hear he's down in Chicago so I'll make my way down there.

MR BURKE. Sir, I admire your initiative and your tenacity and goddamn if there isn't a tear in my eye. And I don't know who this Mr Murphy is but I would like to offer you, right here and right now, my services as a manager – or a partner or...

MRS BURKE. Francis...

MR BURKE. Well why not? It's a business. And if there's one thing I know – it's business.

MRS BURKE. Yes, you know it too well.

MR BURKE. What's that supposed to mean?

MRS BURKE. Well let's just say it's an acquaintanceship that has not treated you and business equally.

MR BURKE. Woman, a man walks in here and I decide to discuss an opportunity – you cannot wait two moments before you deride me!

MRS BURKE takes MR BURKE downstage, away from the others.

MRS BURKE. You can't manage your own son or provide for your wife and you want tell a stranger you'll manage his affairs – with what? From where? Working out of a closet in a two-bit flophouse?!

ELIAS *starts blowing on a harmonica. His parents shout over the din.*

MR BURKE. An operation like this? That's the beauty of it!

MRS BURKE. Beauty's in the eye of the beholder.

MR BURKE. It *is* beautiful! It *is* beautiful! Jesus Christ! Elias! Not at the table!

MR BURKE *slams his hand on the table.*

The band play an underscore of 'Ballad Of A Thin Man'. DR WALKER *addresses us. As he does so, we see* MARIANNE *washing her mother and dressing her.* GENE *helps* MARIANNE *get things ready for the day while the guests drift through the house upstage.*

DR WALKER. Marianne had a lonely upbringing.

To say it wasn't fashionable in Minnesota to bring up a black child in a white family in those days would be an understatement. In 1920, when Marianne was just five years old, three black men named Isaac McGhie, Elmer Jackson and Elias Clayton, were lynched by a mob who broke into the jail, right here in Duluth. Hanged 'em down on the corner of First Street for a crime they hadn't committed. No one was ever even prosecuted for it.

Nick didn't want to be seen holding a little black girl's hand going down to school, so Elizabeth taught her everything she knew right here in the house.

Nick didn't like it one bit when Marianne started going around other parts of the town. Looking for music, for life. But what could he do?

NICK *sits and fixes a drill from his toolbox.*

When Nick was ten years old he was asked to mind his little sister for the day. She was six. Her name was Leonora. This was up in Rocheleau – lotta mining up there. Nick had arranged with his friends to fight another gang of boys up in the woods. He took Leonora with him – she fell down a taconite hole. Fell forty feet. The boys could hear her down there – calling out for Nick. But by the time help came... (*Opens his hands.*) Nick was sent down here to live with his granddaddy. It was one of those stories you hear about people, you think about it every time you look in their face.

MARIANNE *is on the front porch, rolling a cigarette.* GENE *comes out to her, his notebook in hand.*

GENE. Hey.

MARIANNE. Hey.

GENE. Whatcha doin?

MARIANNE. Watchin' the birds.

GENE. What birds?

MARIANNE. The mama and the baby.

GENE. There ain't no babies in November.

MARIANNE. She's got one.

GENE. Maybe it never grew.

MARIANNE. Maybe.

GENE (*pulling his notebook open and scribbling*). No wait that's good. 'The Bird That Never Grew'.

MARIANNE. 'The Bird That Never Grew'?

GENE (*writing*). The Bird That Never Grew.

MARIANNE. Just call it 'The Egg'. You wanna see a movie?

GENE (*dismissive*). Movies. They're so commercial.

MARIANNE. Not like your poems I guess, huh?

GENE. I don't write poems.

MARIANNE. What do you write?

GENE. I write short stories and novellas.

MARIANNE. What's a novella?

GENE. It's an extremely long short story. What's on?

MARIANNE. You see *It Happened One Night*?

GENE. Who's in it?

MARIANNE. Claudette Colbert. It's goofy. This guy is helping this girl run away from getting married.

GENE. You'd go and see it again?

MARIANNE. Sure – if you wanna... I got nothin' to wear.

GENE. You can wear my sweater.

MARIANNE. Right...

GENE. Who's lookin' at you?

MARIANNE pushes him off the bench.

MARIANNE. Well no one I guess!

GENE. I'm kidding! Hey. You ever gonna tell me?

MARIANNE. What.

GENE. You know...

He gestures to her belly.

MARIANNE. Don't ask me, Gene, alright?

They go quiet as NICK *approaches, shoving a list at* MARIANNE.

NICK. Here – take this down to Maroutha's.

MARIANNE. I can't! He says you owe him ninety dollars!

NICK. Jesus! Here. (*He gives her some money.*) So Gene...

MARIANNE. This is seven dollars!

NICK. I'll get him the rest later! So Gene – (*Suddenly seeing* GENE*'s black eye.*) The hell happened to your face?

GENE. Someone thought I had their lottery ticket.

NICK. Did ya?

GENE. I wish!

NICK *gives* GENE *a letter*.

What's this?

NICK. Read it.

GENE. What is it?

NICK (*going*). Appointment for an interview.

GENE. Interview for what?

NICK. Lake Superior and Mississippi Railroad. Right here.

GENE. Yeah, what is it? Punching tickets?

NICK (*coming back*). What do you care? You know what other guys'd do just to get in the door? Just to sweep the damn platform? I ain't gonna tell you the favors I had to pull. Had to sweet-talk an old girlfriend.

GENE. I don't wanna hear that!

NICK. You kids don't think I was young once? You think I was born like this? Like an old man!

MARIANNE. I never even considered it.

NICK (*going*). Well – you have no idea, my friend.

GENE. Yeah, well that's got nothin' to do with me.

NICK (*coming back*). No, huh? And I got nothin' to do with you?

GENE. Mostly you don't.

NICK (*offended*). I don't have nothing to do with you?

GENE. Why the sudden interest?

NICK. I can't take an interest in you?

GENE. Sure, I guess.

NICK. Well there you go.

GENE. What you up to?

NICK. I'm not up to nothing.

GENE. I don't get it.

NICK. I want for you to make money.

GENE. Alright.

NICK. You get it?

GENE. Yes.

NICK. You do this for me, okay? You do it for me, you do it for your mother, you do your best. What?

GENE. Nothing.

MARIANNE. Do it for your poems.

GENE. I don't write poems.

NICK. Hm?

GENE *and* MARIANNE. Nothing!

MARIANNE. What?

NICK. Nothing! You go to that interview.

    NICK *turns to go and sees a girl of about twenty standing there, dressed for travel, with an umbrella.*

    Morning, Kate.

KATE. Morning, Mr Laine. Morning, Marianne.

MARIANNE. Morning.

NICK. How's your mother?

KATE. Well, thank you.

NICK. And your father?

KATE. He's not so good.

NICK. I'm sorry to hear that. Will you excuse me please? (*To* GENE.) Do it for Kate.

MARIANNE (*sotto to* GENE). Do it for Kate.

    NICK *and* MARIANNE *go*.

GENE. Kate…

KATE. Do what?

GENE. Nothing.

KATE. I hope it's alright – calling by like this.

GENE. No! Hey... Come in.

KATE. I can't stay.

GENE. Hey, that's alright. You want some breakfast?

KATE. No, thank you, I'm fine.

GENE. Cup of coffee?

KATE. I can't. I have a ticket for the nine o'clock Greyhound – to Boston.

GENE. You going to Boston?

KATE. I got a job. Teaching. For a family. It's kind of a governess.

GENE. Great.

KATE. Three girls – and they have goats.

GENE. Wow. That's terrif...

KATE. Jed Simons has asked me to marry him, Gene. I've said yes.

GENE. Wo... Wow that's... That's great.

KATE. I wanted to tell you myself. You know how these things...

GENE. I know. That's... That can be really... thank you.

KATE. Are you okay?

GENE. I'm great. I'm... Why wouldn't I...?

KATE. What happened to your face?

GENE. Oh this! No, I... Damn branch on that sycamore tree sprung back and hit me while was, tryna... chop it down.

KATE (*looking at his face, concerned*). Did you clean it?

GENE. I gotta clean it. I'll do it.

KATE. If I had time I'd...

She approaches him. He backs away.

GENE. No, no, I know, I'll do it. I know. So, Boston!

KATE. Yeah.

GENE. That's great.

KATE. Yeah it's… You know Jed is gonna be working out there.

GENE. Yeah, I heard something… That's…

KATE. Gene, I'm sorry about what I said to you…

GENE. When?

KATE. You know…

GENE. Oh, hey, no. Don't. I deserved it.

KATE. I do admire you, Gene. I always have. And nobody loves your stories more than I do. Just when I read that really long one and that one thing about that girl, I guess I got angry and I said some things I didn't really mean and then, when no one could find you…

GENE. Kate, I was drunk.

KATE. Okay…

GENE. I was drunk and I… You know what? When we're old and we're like fifty years old and we look back at this whole thing, you know what? I bet we're just gonna laugh our damn heads off about the whole thing. I'm even laughing right now. It's funny!

KATE. I better go, Gene.

GENE. You better go, Kate. And you know what?

KATE. Yeah?

GENE. Nothin'.

KATE *starts to go, she turns back.*

KATE. I wanted to give you back this, Gene. I nearly forgot. It's your mother's St Christopher medal.

GENE. Keep it.

KATE. No I couldn't.

GENE. Really.

KATE. It's your mother's.

GENE. No keep it. Really. She won't care.

KATE. I couldn't.

GENE (*losing his temper*). I said keep it! I said keep it! (*He shoves it roughly in her hand.*) I don't want it. You understand me? I don't want it!

KATE, *confused, holds on to it and moves away. Bare chords for 'I Want You' begin under the following.*

I'll see you, Kate. You take care.

KATE. Okay.

GENE (*calls to her*). I have an interview.

KATE (*turning*). Oh?

GENE. Yeah, Lake Superior and Mississippi Railroad.

KATE. Oh that's wonderful.

GENE. Yeah. They say I should be making three thousand dollars by this time next year.

KATE. Really?

GENE. Sure.

KATE *doesn't really believe him, but smiles and starts to go.*

You wanna see the letter?

KATE. No that's fine.

GENE. You tell Jed!

KATE. I will.

She turns away and leaves.

I Want You

GENE.
 The guilty undertaker sighs
 The lonesome organ grinder cries
 The silver saxophones say I should refuse you

The cracked bells and washed-out horns
Blow into my face with scorn
But it's not that way
I wasn't born to lose you

I want you, I want you
I want you so bad
Honey, I want you

KATE *and* GENE.

The drunken politician leaps
Upon the street where mothers weep
And the saviors who are fast asleep, they wait for you
And I wait for them to interrupt
Me drinkin' from my broken cup
And ask me to
Open up the gate for you

I want you, I want you
I want you so bad
Honey, I want you

KATE.

How all my fathers, they've gone down
True love they've been without it
But all their daughters put me down
'Cause I don't think about it

KATE *and* GENE.

Well, I return to the Queen of Spades
And talk with my chambermaid
She knows that I'm not afraid to look at her
She is good to me
And there's nothing she doesn't see
She knows where I'd like to be
But it doesn't matter

I want you, I want you
I want you so bad
Honey, I want you

A capella:

I want you, I want you, I want you...

MARLOWE *comes into the dining room.* ELIZABETH *is there.*

ELIZABETH. So you're God's representative on Earth, huh?

MARLOWE. Oh no… I'm a mere servant of the servant. Can I serve you?

ELIZABETH. You can't scratch this itch, Padre. I been a long time on the prairie.

MARLOWE. Well you let me know. What you keep all down in here, under your seat there?

ELIZABETH. It's an escape hatch.

MARLOWE. I see.

ELIZABETH. Day's gonna come we all gotta blow.

MARLOWE. Well maybe you'll show me the way out.

ELIZABETH. Everybody gotta go a different door, Monsignor.

MARLOWE. Well maybe that's so.

ELIZABETH. You get a wash this morning?

MARLOWE. Well of course.

ELIZABETH. You might need to go another rinse. It don't smell so sweet down here in the downwind.

MARLOWE. Well perhaps I need to find a laundry.

ELIZABETH. Yeah, well you find a good one. I don't need no louses. I seen one walking down the parting in my hair when I was fixing myself one day. There he was just strolling along the white-line parting like it was a nice country lane, as peaceful and serene… I knew it then, Lord Jesus, I knew it then. I wasn't coming back. (*Beat.*) I can see a louse. I can see 'em.

MARLOWE. Oh can you now?

ELIZABETH. Why yes I can.

ELIAS *has wandered in alone.* MARLOWE *goes to him.*

MARLOWE. Let me show you something. Hello, Elias. I farm out where the crippled voices heal. Watch this…

He guides ELIAS *downstage to sit and laughs a little, to* ELIZABETH.

You're makin' me nervous now.

He closes his eyes and holds a hand over ELIAS*'s head to heal him.*

(*Whispering*.) Sweet Jesus, sweet Jesus, sweet Jesus, sweet Jesus, sweet Jesus, sweet Jesus...

ELIZABETH *sings 'Farther Along' and comes to sit with* ELIAS.

ELIZABETH.
When we see Jesus coming in glory
When he comes down from his home in the sky.
Then we shall meet Him in that bright mansion
We'll understand it all by and by.

MARLOWE *now has his hand over* ELIZAETH*'s head too. She wheels round on him.*

(*Speaking*.) Wait a minute! Are you doin' me?

MARLOWE. No!

ELIZABETH. You are! You're doin' me! I don't need doin'! I don't need your stinky Jesus.

MR BURKE *comes in, carrying a fishing rod and a bag with fishing gear.*

MARLOWE. You going fishing? Looks cold out there!

MR BURKE. Elias likes to try. We hardly ever catch anything. Once or twice we had some supper out of it.

One of the guides on the rod is missing. MR BURKE *finds a little wire in a bowl to fix it.*

MARLOWE. That's a fine boy you got there, Mr Burke.

MR BURKE. Thank you. He's a handful. Aren't you?

ELIAS. You gotta ah, ah, ah, put seaweed in the jar so the fish can breathe.

MR BURKE. That's right. It's what we do anyway. Bits of grass, you know.

MARLOWE (*helping* MR BURKE *to fix the rod*). Sweet. That's very sweet. You plan on putting some roots down here or you just passing through?

MR BURKE. I guess we'll be moving on. I came down here chasing a debtor gave me the runaround. Everybody chasing everybody else. You know how it is.

MARLOWE. You have creditors on your heels too?

MR BURKE. Everybody got to wait in line, just like everybody else.

MARLOWE. What direction you blowin' in from?

MR BURKE. North.

MARLOWE. North?

MR BURKE. North-west.

MARLOWE. Lotta nice places up there, Wolf Point, Medina. (*Pronounced 'Medeena'*.)

MR BURKE *and* ELIZABETH. Medina. (*Pronounced 'Med-dine-uh'*.)

MARLOWE (*correcting himself*). Medina, Medina...

ELIZABETH. Some people say vageena.

MARLOWE. I spent time up in your neck of the woods.

MR BURKE. Uh-huh?

MARLOWE. Wasn't much hunger for the word, but by Christ were they ravenous for something just the same!

MR BURKE. I guess.

Through the following, we hear underscore for 'Blind Willie McTell'.

MARLOWE. Yes it was last spring. I heard a terrible story.
About a poor girl's getting attacked up in the woods.
Suspicion fell here and there. Some said this, some said that.
Someone even said maybe it was a man or child didn't know their own strength. Maybe was a little feeble in his mind.
Who can say? You know how it is with rumors. A family by the name of Shepherd. You hear anything about that?

MR BURKE. No, can't say I have.

MARLOWE. These things can happen so easily. I once officiated at a funeral for an infant whose own mother had crushed him to death with an overly fervent embrace. Can you imagine?

MR BURKE. That's terrible.

MARLOWE. Life is terrible.

MR BURKE. It sure can be.

MARLOWE. But you and your wife seem united. And that's the main thing, I guess.

MR BURKE. What you driving at?

MARLOWE. I ain't out to cause trouble. World's already full of trouble. But like they say there's a man going round with his wife and his grown son saying he lost his business. Maybe that's just what he's saying. Maybe he's been moving round 'cause he's got something to hide.

MR BURKE. You're in the wrong garden, preacher. (*Heading out.*) Come on, Elias! Couple up!

MARLOWE. Maybe. But I got to be where I am. Just like the next man. Five hundred dollars should do it. Say twelve o'clock, tomorrow. You meet me here, fine. If not, I'll call by the precinct. Just tell 'em what I know. Look at that! Sun's coming out.

MR BURKE *grabs* MARLOWE.

MR BURKE. Now you listen to me, you son of a bitch. You want to threaten people, you want to get your due, I'll give it to you. You so much as say a goddamn word about me to anyone, I'll cut your fucking throat. You keep your lies to yourself. I don't know a damn thing what you're talking about.

MARLOWE *screeches a loud 'Whooooeeee!', embracing* MR BURKE, *who backs away, startled.*

MARLOWE. Then what you getting so riled up about for then, huh? Good day. I'm famished. Twelve o'clock tomorrow. May your catch be bountiful, Elias.

MARLOWE *leaves*. MR BURKE *angrily takes the fishing rod from* ELIAS.

MR BURKE. What you doing? Gimme that! Look! You took 'em all off! Goddamn...

ELIAS *suddenly rushes at* MR BURKE, *forcing him on to the table, choking him.* MR BURKE *is completely silent, unable to get a breath as he struggles in the eerie quiet.*
ELIZABETH *is fixing her make-up. Finally* ELIAS *releases* MR BURKE.

Hey, that's alright. Daddy didn't mean to shout. I'm sorry. I love you. Come on, we go fishing, huh? Come on.

BURKE *leads* ELIAS *out.* ELIZABETH *sings.*

Like A Rolling Stone

ELIZABETH.
> Once upon a time you dressed so fine
> You threw the bums a dime in your prime, didn't you?
> People'd call, say, 'Beware doll, you're bound to fall'
> You thought they were all kiddin' you
> You used to laugh about
> Everybody that was hangin' out
> Now you don't talk so loud
> Now you don't seem so proud
> About having to be scrounging for your next meal
>
> How does it feel
> How does it feel
> To be without a home
> Like a complete unknown
> Like a rolling stone?
>
> You've gone to the finest school all right, Miss Lonely
> But you know you only used to get juiced in it
> And nobody has ever taught you how to live on the street
> And now you find out you're gonna have to get used to it
> You said you'd never compromise
> With the mystery tramp, but now you realize
> He's not selling any alibis

As you stare into the vacuum of his eyes
And ask him do you want to make a deal?

How does it feel
How does it feel
To be on your own
With no direction home
Like a complete unknown
Like a rolling stone?

A trio of the female company segue into 'Make You Feel My Love':

FEMALE ENSEMBLE.
The storms are raging on the rollin' sea
And on the highway of regret
The winds of change are blowing wild and free
You ain't seen nothing like me yet.

I could make you happy, make your dreams come true
There is nothing that I wouldn't do
Go to the ends of the earth for you
To make you feel my...

SCOTT *comes and takes a jug, pours some water in a bowl. He looks beat up. He moves gingerly, feeling his rib is cracked. He dabs at his face and his knuckles.* ELIZABETH *stands with him.*

MARIANNE *comes in and stands watching him from the shadows.*

MARIANNE. Hey, tough guy. I saw you fighting.

SCOTT. You saw me get beat.

MARIANNE. I thought you had him.

SCOTT. Me too. That's how he got me.

MARIANNE. At least you got beat by a gentleman. He shook your hand after.

SCOTT. That handshake hurt me more than all the times he hit me. He knew it, too. How'd you know about the fight?

MARIANNE. My friend Ria. She saw a poster, but you had a different name. They let us stand in the back.

SCOTT. I wish you hadn't.

MARIANNE *takes some dressing, pouring some whiskey on it. She gently lifts* SCOTT*'s face to the light and starts cleaning him up.*

MARIANNE. Look at you. Boxing's so foolish. They say that in the Bible you know.

SCOTT. Yeah?

MARIANNE. Leviticus. Chapter three, verse four.

SCOTT. What?

MARIANNE. I'm making it up. You can say anything is in Leviticus.

ELIZABETH. I like boxing.

MARIANNE. Mama.

ELIZABETH. I like boxers. I like you.

SCOTT *winces as* MARIANNE *dabs at his face.*

MARIANNE. Stop fussing! I'm nursing you back to health, goddamnit.

ELIZABETH. Goddamnit.

SCOTT. How far are you along?

She looks at him. Looks away.

MARIANNE. Four and a half months. Say five.

SCOTT. Where's the daddy?

MARIANNE. Working the boats.

SCOTT. You gonna get married?

MARIANNE. You believe in marriage?

SCOTT. Sure. You don't?

MARIANNE. You either love somebody or you don't. Marriage don't got nothing to do with it.

SCOTT. It's not too late to… I mean… You don't have to have it.

MARIANNE. At five months?

SCOTT. Depends who you ask. Where you go.

MARIANNE (*changing the subject*). When you going to Chicago?

SCOTT. Tomorrow. Day after. Soon as I get me some dough. You do a deal with the pier man. He'll find you somewhere on board. You just stay out of the way. It's alright.

MARIANNE. You think I'd like Chicago, huh?

SCOTT. Chicago rises up off the plain like a magical kingdom when you see it first, I swear. And then... well, you go inside and they'll rob you kill you if you don't mind your business. But stay with someone who knows what they're doing?

He shadow-boxes. MARIANNE *puts her hands up, joining in for a moment before walking away.*

MARIANNE. Oh, like you?

SCOTT. Wait! That's how you box?

MARIANNE. I don't box! I never had to fight.

SCOTT. You always get everything you ask for.

MARIANNE. It's better than looking like you.

SCOTT *offers to show her how to box.*

SCOTT. Come here.

MARIANNE *smiles and joins him, taking his instruction.*

(*Demonstrates.*) Wide stance like this. Wider. Get grounded. Put your hands up like this. Chin down, close the barn doors.

MARIANNE. I can't see.

SCOTT. You gotta protect your face. You right-handed?

MARIANNE. Mm-hm.

SCOTT. Swivel your right foot, turn from the hip and gimme one jab right here.

MARIANNE *tries to hit* SCOTT*'s hand, but misses. He laughs.*

MARIANNE. What?

SCOTT. No, that's amazing, that's really good. Let's try the left. Gimme two right here. That's right. Now do it like you hate me.

MARIANNE. That won't be hard.

She lands a solid punch in his palm.

SCOTT. There you go!

SCOTT raises his hands in triumph. MARIANNE surprises him with a jab to his broken rib. He recoils.

MARIANNE. That's how you got beat, Mr Chicago. You're too nice.

SCOTT. You're dangerous!

ELIZABETH. She is. She was born dangerous.

SCOTT. I'll show you who to ask down on the pier, you want to go. You think about it. You let me know.

ELIZABETH. Are you married, Joe?

MARIANNE. Mama.

SCOTT. Excuse me, ma'am?

ELIZABETH. It's a simple question. It's my life. And if I want to spend the rest of it with this...

SCOTT. What did she say?

MARIANNE. Are you married, Mr Scott?

SCOTT. Yes I am. I got me a wife and two children. But I ain't seen 'em for a long time. My wife is with another man. I don't want to cause 'em all no trouble.

He hides his pain around this issue, but MARIANNE has seen it.

MARIANNE. Alright. You know, you wouldn't believe me if I told you the truth.

SCOTT. About what?

MARIANNE. About my baby.

SCOTT. You don't have to tell me a damn thing.

NICK *comes in. He senses the intimacy between* SCOTT *and* MARIANNE.

NICK. Watcha doin'?

MARIANNE. Cleaning up.

NICK. Get your momma some supper.

MARIANNE. Come on, Momma.

ELIZABETH. We going to the movies?

MARIANNE. Sure.

NICK *looks at* SCOTT.

NICK. You okay?

SCOTT. Yes, sir.

NICK. Ha?

SCOTT. I'm fine.

NICK. Alright.

SCOTT *goes.*

(*To* MARIANNE.) You speak with Mr Perry last night?

MARIANNE *continues her work.*

You know he came all the way up here for that talk. You talk with him?

MARIANNE. Sure.

NICK. What did he say? He say anything?

MARIANNE. Sure.

NICK. Well that's… Did you… what did you…

MARIANNE. Nothin'.

NICK. Nothin'. What do you mean, nothin'? He brought you up them nice flowers, you didn't say nothing to him?

MARIANNE. Were those flowers for me?

NICK. Yeah!

MARIANNE. Well he took 'em with him.

NICK. What you mean?

MARIANNE. If they were for me he never said. He took them with him.

NICK. Well that's... Were you civil to him?

MARIANNE (*affronted*). What do you think I am?

NICK. That's a question! I'm not sure I rightly know! Stand still for one second. What you discuss? You didn't discuss nothing?

MARIANNE. Looks like all the discussin's already been done.

NICK. What are you talkin' about?

MARIANNE. He told me you and him already got it all planned out.

NICK. We may have... spoken. I may have answered some... I spoke with him, but it's... No one is saying you ain't got to want this for yourself.

MARIANNE. What could possibly make you think this is something I want? What you want make me go for?!

NICK. You think this is what I want? When I went down to Burnsville for my uncle's funeral – all along the whole street into the town – people living in tents. In tents! In the United States of America! Kids with no clothes on. People sitting out in the rain, lining up for a bowl of soup. There ain't no net to catch us, Marianne.

MARIANNE. Why don't you let me help you?

NICK. When I needed your help was when I needed you to be a good girl. That was when you coulda helped me.

MARIANNE. Daddy, I didn't...

NICK. Don't give me that cock-and-bull story. You gotta go carrying on with some goddamn boatman?! Like some little whore?!

MRS NEILSEN *has come through*. MARIANNE *leaves*.

What the hell you doin' wasting your life away in here for?

MRS NEILSEN. I gotta waste it somewhere.

She comes to NICK *and takes his hand. He doesn't really respond. She goes and sits.*

ELIZABETH *is singing…*

Like A Rolling Stone

ELIZABETH.
>How does it feel
>How does it feel
>To be on your own
>With no direction home

The band coming in softly underneath her. Over this the rest of the cast are harmonizing with…

I Want You

ALL.
>I want you
>I want you
>I want you
>So bad
>Honey I want you…

ELIZABETH.
>Like a rolling stone.

NICK *sits disconsolately, until* MARIANNE *comes in and takes* ELIZABETH *out.*

Black.

ACT TWO

What Can I Do For You?

FEMALE ENSEMBLE MEMBER.
> You have given everything to me
> What can I do for You?
> You have given me eyes to see
> What can I do for You?

MR BURKE.
> Pulled me out of bondage and You made me renewed inside
> Filled up a hunger that had always been denied
> You opened up a door no man can shut and You opened it
>   up so wide
> And You've chosen me to be among the few

ALL.
> What can I do for You?

SCOTT.
> I know all about poison, I know all about fiery darts
> I don't care how rough the road is, show me where it starts
> Whatever pleases You, tell it to my heart
> Well, I don't deserve it but I sure did make it through

ALL.
> What can I do for You?

The company segues into:

You Ain't Goin' Nowhere

ALL.
> Clouds so swift
> Rain won't lift
> Gate won't close
> Railings froze
> Get your mind off wintertime

You ain't goin' nowhere
Whoo-ee! Ride me high Tomorrow's the day
My bride's gonna come
Oh, oh, are we gonna fly
Down in the easy chair!

I don't care
How many letters they sent
Morning came and morning went
Pick up your money
And pack up your tent
You ain't goin' nowhere Whoo-ee!
Ride me high
Tomorrow's the day
My bride's gonna come
Oh, oh, are we gonna fly
Down in the easy chair!

Buy me a flute
And a gun that shoots
Tailgates and substitutes
Strap yourself
To the tree with roots
You ain't goin' nowhere
Whoo-ee! Ride me high
Tomorrow's the day
My bride's gonna come
Oh, oh, are we gonna fly
Down in the easy chair!

Genghis Khan
He could not keep
All his kings
Supplied with sleep
We'll climb that hill no matter how steep
When we get up to it
Whoo-ee! Ride me high
Tomorrow's the day
My bride's gonna come
Oh, oh, are we gonna fly
Down in the easy chair!

They segue into 'Jokerman':

Jokerman

FULL FEMALE ENSEMBLE.
> Standing on the waters casting your bread
> While the eyes of the idol with the iron head are glowing
> Distant ships sailing into the mist
> You were born with a snake in both of your fists while a
> > hurricane was blowing
> Freedom just around the corner for you
> But with the truth so far off, what good will it do?

> Jokerman dance to the nightingale tune
> Bird fly high by the light of the moon
> Oh, oh, oh, Jokerman

A party is in full swing upstage. Some shadowy figures in the lamplight, singing or dancing or talking, playing cards. ELIZABETH *is dancing with* ELIAS. MR BURKE *is drinking and playing cards with* MRS NEILSEN.

DR WALKER *addresses us.*

DR WALKER. It's Wednesday November 21st 1934. The night before Thanksgiving. The last one we ever celebrated together.

MRS BURKE. You got anymore drops?

He gives her a little bottle, she takes some.

DR WALKER. Keep it.

MRS BURKE. You sure?

DR WALKER. Six drops a day maximum.

MRS BURKE. Thank you.

DR WALKER. You don't want to become addicted.

MRS BURKE. Too late!

He looks at her.

I'm kidding! Of course not. Six drops. You must have a nice house, Doctor.

DR WALKER. I have a nice house, but I only live in two rooms. I eat in one, I sleep in the other.

MRS BURKE. You what in the other?

DR WALKER. I sleep! I sleep!

MRS. BURKE. We had a house bigger than this one, you know.

DR WALKER. I'm sure you did.

MRS BURKE. How would it be, do you think, if I came to your house someday? I only say this for conversation.

DR WALKER. Well I'm sure that would be very pleasant.

MRS BURKE. You think? I think it would be really sad. If we coupled, I mean. We'd be like two lonely beasts in the field. And yet...

DR WALKER. Yes.

MRS BURKE. Yes?

DR WALKER. We wouldn't be lonely.

ELIZABETH. You'll still be lonely. You'll always be lonely. But you should still do it!

They laugh.

MRS BURKE *is attending to* ELIAS.

DR WALKER. This time of year, a lost soul could always find a welcome up here. Suicide had increased by nearly one hundred percent in the years after the crash. Single men led the way, followed closely by divorced women. My own marriage had failed in the years before. I say it failed, but really I failed. A little morphine helped – until it didn't. I weaned myself off of it.

ELIZABETH. Mostly.

DR WALKER. Mostly.

MR BURKE *lurches downstage towards* DR WALKER, *taking his glass of bourbon and hand of cards with him.*

MR BURKE. Hey, Doc! I heard your good buddy Franklin Dingaling Snoozevelt on the wireless this evening!

DR WALKER. I thought you might!

MR BURKE. You do know what it is we really need, dontcha? In the White House? A strong man.

MRS NEILSEN. Yes! Like FDR.

MR BURKE. I'm sick of hearing 'FDR is a good man' this and 'FDR is a good man' that.

MR BURKE *playfully tussles with* ELIAS.

DR WALKER (*laughs*). Sorry to hear that, Frank.

MR BURKE. I couldn't care less if he's yay or nay or rollin' in the hay. Long as the head man is strong I don't care two sausages if he's any good. 'Cause what we need is energy.

ELIZABETH. Energy!

MR BURKE. That's right, Mrs Laine! Energy – not morals!!

ELIZABETH. Woo-hoo!!

MRS NEILSEN *follows* MR BURKE *and takes his cards from his hand.*

MRS NEILSEN. That's my trick! Two dollars!

MR BURKE. Oh Jesus. Here you go.

MRS NEILSEN. Thank you. You want another game? Double or nothing?

MR BURKE. No – Jesus! Energy!

ELIZABETH. Energy!

MR BURKE (*wrestling with* ELIAS). You know. Just someone doin' something – even if it's the wrong thing. People start gettin' ideas. Start feelin' like they can do somethin' about it. Put what they know to good use. That's all you need to get the ball rolling.

MRS NEILSEN *pours herself a drink.*

MRS NEILSEN. I don't know about that. People say there can't be no more wars now 'cause we all know it's no good. We don't know shit if you ask me. Excuse my language.

MR BURKE. I like your language.

MRS NEILSEN. Everybody gotta make their *own* mistakes and anyone thinks we don't is a fuckin' banana. Excuse my language.

MR BURKE. I like your language! 'Anyone who thinks we won't *is* a fuckin' banana.'

MRS BURKE (*to* MR BURKE). You're a fuckin' banana.

She spots NICK *coming through to talk with* DR WALKER.

Oh Nick!

NICK. How are you this evening, Mrs Burke?

MRS BURKE (*straight in, privately*). Nick, I have to ask you if we can extend our credit.

NICK. In which direction?

MRS BURKE. Francis has an old partner down in Rush City who has six hundred dollars he's been waiting to pay him. It's just a question of the weather, you see. It's tricky getting down there.

NICK. The weather, huh? When do you think it's gonna...

MRS BURKE. Nick. I know we owe you.

NICK. It's alright.

MRS BURKE *suddenly puts her face in her hands, hiding her tears.*

Come on now.

NICK *puts an arm round her.*

MRS BURKE (*a rush of words*). If my mother saw me here now, she'd die. She'd be so ashamed. Is your mother still alive, Nick?

NICK. I hope not.

MRS BURKE. Why?

NICK. 'Cause we buried her fifteen years ago.

MRS BURKE *can't help laughing.* MRS NEILSEN *comes to* MRS BURKE *and takes her to get a drink.*

NICK *comes to* DR WALKER *and* ELIZABETH.

NICK. Hey, Doc, latest is she says she hears stuff.

DR WALKER. Hears what?

NICK. A girl down a hole.

DR WALKER. Okay.

NICK. I know who it is. That's the... That's the... [crazy thing.]

DR WALKER. You were a kid, Nick. You were just a kid.

MARIANNE *is dancing with* SCOTT. *She collides with* DR WALKER.

MARIANNE. Oh! Sorry!

DR WALKER *pulls* NICK *downstage for a private word.*

DR WALKER. Nick – You know what pseudocyesis is?

NICK. Pseudo-what?

DR WALKER. Cyesis.

NICK. What is it?

DR WALKER. Well, sometimes if a girl feels an intense need to... connect or to... well, to have a baby. Her body can manifest all the signs of a real pregnancy.

Just then, MR PERRY *comes in, holding his bunch of flowers.*

MR PERRY. Dr Walker.

DR WALKER. Mr Perry. Right, well, I'll...

DR WALKER *leaves.*

NICK. What.

MR PERRY. I didn't say anything.

NICK. What.

MR PERRY. Nothing.

NICK. I can feel it. What.

MR PERRY. No, I...

NICK. Yeah?

Fireworks go off outside, attracting everyone outside except for NICK, ELIZABETH *and* MR PERRY.

MR PERRY. I just feel like I'm… It's almost like I'm getting to where you're making me beg.

NICK. Beg?

MR PERRY. Yet I'm the one doing *you* a favor!

NICK. I'm not asking you to do a damn thing. What do you want me to do?

MR PERRY. Maybe ask her to come down to my store, will ya?

NICK. She won't go down to your store.

MR PERRY. Then what am I doing here?

MR PERRY *starts to go,* NICK *stops him.*

NICK. No, wait. You just say, 'Let's go and talk and…'

MR PERRY. We've talked. I've talked to her.

NICK. Talk to her again. Lay it out.

MR PERRY. You lay it out.

NICK. I've laid it out! Now you lay it out!

MR PERRY. Jesus. What the fuck is happening to me? How do we ever think any of the crazy shit we do is a good idea? I mean, how does that happen? Who's pulling the strings?

ELIZABETH *(suddenly lucid)*. Then find someone your own age. You old goat.

MR PERRY *(rounds on her angrily)*. You don't think I've tried? You don't think I want that? How do you do it? Where do you go? I talk to women who come in my store – in that way – what would people say?

NICK. Just be friendly.

MR PERRY *(angrily)*. I'm friendly! I'm friendly, Nick. People just take it the wrong way!

NICK. That's why this gives you an advantage.

MR PERRY. How?

NICK. 'Cause you're *helping* her. You're helping *me*. Feel good, Mr Perry. Joe. Can I call you Joe?

MR PERRY. No.

NICK. Feel good, Mr Perry.

MR PERRY. May I use your water closet?

NICK. My what?

MR PERRY. Water closet. Your honey bucket.

NICK. Oh sure. Right around there. Through the kitchen.

MR PERRY. Thank you. You know what? I'm... gonna go for a walk, look at the fireworks.

He goes.

NICK. You do that. (*Sotto.*) And don't hurry back.

NICK *starts to tidy up.*

ELIZABETH. Well, Nick.

NICK *ignores her.*

Well, Nick.

NICK. What.

ELIZABETH. Just well, Nick.

NICK (*not very interested*). Mm-hm?

ELIZABETH. You think I don't see? You think I don't *give* a good goddamn? You don't think I give a good wocky-woo?

NICK. Elizabeth, I don't know what you give or what you get.

ELIZABETH. Yeah, whaddya whaddya whaddya whaddya whaddya.

NICK. What.

ELIZABETH. Shut up.

NICK. You have to be rude?

ELIZABETH. You think this is rude? You ain't seen rude. You think I care? Huh? About your little lady woman up in your attic. (*As though talking to a child, patronisingly.*) It's alright, Nicky Wicky. Animals got to feel the warm, right? I'mma not care one way or tother nother.

NICK. So what you so angry about then? You don't think I do enough? You don't think I couldn't get you put away in some old ladies' home like that – (*Snaps fingers.*)

ELIZABETH. You're too mean.

NICK. They'd take you away. Nobody would say I haven't put up with enough fucking crap. Offa you. Offa everybody.

ELIZABETH. Oh boo boo boo, boo boo boo boo, poor boo.

NICK. Elizabeth, I swear to God I'll knock your damn teeth in.

ELIZABETH. Oh knock my deed in. You'll knock my deed in. How much money you get?

NICK. Money where?

ELIZABETH. Off a the money man. The shoe man.

NICK. What money? He's sick! He ain't gonna last a year!

ELIZABETH. Whatcha have to stick her in his old dirty bed for?

NICK. Girl needs help. Whatcha want? You want her goin' round the roads? Dragging her baby? Tramping in the dirt? I ain't got nothin' for her.

ELIZABETH. Be like sleeping in a damn grave – his cold feet like clay comin' round her. At least in a whorehouse she can name her own price. You hear the girl down the hole?

NICK. What?

ELIZABETH. I know you hear it.

NICK. Why don't you shut your fucking mouth?

ELIZABETH. I know you do. You hear it more than me!

NICK *suddenly grabs* ELIZABETH. *She fights him.*

You do! You do! You do!

NICK. I don't hear nothing! I don't hear a damn thing! Shut up!
You hear me? You shut up!

ELIZABETH *pulls away, she puts her hands to her face.*
NICK *stands there looking helplessly at her.*

I'm sorry. Elizabeth. I'm sorry alright?

Sweetheart Like You

MRS BURKE.
Well, the pressure's down, the boss ain't here
He's gone North, he ain't around
They say that vanity got the best of him
But he sure left here in style
By the way, that's a cute hat
And that smile's so hard to resist
But what's a sweetheart like you doin' in a dump like this?

You know, I once knew a woman who looked like you
She wanted a whole man, not just a half
She used to call me sweet daddy when I was only a child
You kind of remind me of her when you laugh
In order to deal in this game, got to make the queen disappear
It's done with a flick of the wrist
But what's a sweetheart like you doin' in a dump like this?

MRS BURKE *and* MRS NEILSEN.
You know you can make a name for yourself
You can hear them tires squeal
You can be known as the most beautiful woman
Who ever crawled across cut glass to make a deal

We segue into:

True Love Tends To Forget

MRS NEILSEN.
I'm getting weary looking in my baby's eyes
When she's near me she's so hard to recognize
I finally realize there's no room for regret
True love, true love, true love tends to forget

Hold me, baby be near
You told me that you'd be sincere
Every day of the year's like playin' Russian roulette
True love, true love, true love tends to forget

I was lyin' down in the reeds without any oxygen
I saw you in the wilderness among the men
Saw you drift into infinity and come back again
All you got to do is wait and I'll tell you when

Underscore...

(*Speaking.*) I'm gonna go, Nick. I can't pay you no more.

NICK. What are you talking about?

MRS NEILSEN. I went to see Mr St Clair about signing all the forms.

NICK. When?

MRS NEILSEN. Today.

NICK. Yeah?

MRS NEILSEN. Turns out I owe him money.

NICK. You'll pay him when you get your inheritance.

MRS NEILSEN. The legal fees ate it all up! There ain't nothing for me or anyone else.

NICK. You're kidding me. That goddamn crook! I'm gonna go down there myself and I'll...

MRS NEILSEN. He showed me the figures, Nick. It was all there in black and white.

NICK. You're kidding me...

MRS NEILSEN. I know you need the room. I'll clear out.

NICK. What?! Where?

MRS NEILSEN. My sister.

NICK. In Minneapolis?

MRS NEILSEN. No, my twin sister. In Oklahoma.

NICK. Oklahoma?! Are you nuts?!

MRS NEILSEN. Oklahoma City. She's married to a schoolteacher.

NICK (*sarcastic*). Oh! Right!

MRS NEILSEN. She can put me up for a while.

NICK (*exasperated*). Right.

MRS NEILSEN. Maybe find me some work out there.

NICK. Yeah.

MRS NEILSEN. We ain't gonna buy no hotel, Nick.

NICK. Huh. It's all over I guess.

MRS NEILSEN. Don't speak like that. Do you love me?

NICK. What?

MRS NEILSEN. Can you love me?

NICK. What kind of question is that?

MRS NEILSEN. I can take it either way. But you gotta tell me the truth.

NICK. You just said it's all bullshit!

MRS NEILSEN. Yeah it's all bullshit. It's still all I got!

NICK. We ain't spring chickens.

MRS NEILSEN. What's that gotta do with it?

NICK. You live too long, you see too much. It chips away at you. How can you love someone who ain't got a soul?

MRS NEILSEN. You have a soul.

NICK. I don't feel it.

MRS NEILSEN. I feel it. Just say it to me. Just say it.

NICK. I can't love anyone! There it is! There's the truth!

MRS NEILSEN. Can't or won't?

She sings 'True Love Tends To Forget'.

> I was lyin' down in the reeds without any oxygen
> I saw you in the wilderness among the men
> Saw you drift into infinity and come back again
> All you got to do is wait and I'll tell you when
>
> You belong to me, baby, without any doubt
> Don't forsake me, baby, don't sell me out
> Don't keep me knockin' about from Mexico to Tibet
> True love, true love, true love tends to forget

We segue back into 'Sweetheart Like You':

MRS BURKE.
> They say that patriotism is the last refuge
> To which a scoundrel clings
> Steal a little and they throw you in jail
> Steal a lot and they make you king
> There's only one step down from here, baby
> It's called the land of permanent bliss
> What's a sweetheart like you doin' in a dump like this?

It's the next day. MR PERRY has returned with his wilted-looking flowers.

MR PERRY. Happy Thanksgiving, Nick.

NICK *(startled)*. Jesus Christ! Yeah – Happy Thanksgiving, Mr Perry. You been out here all night? Look at you, you're freezing! Get inside.

NICK *drags him inside.*

MR PERRY. Happy Thanksgiving, Elizabeth.

NICK. Get in here.

MARIANNE *is sitting with* ELIZABETH. NICK *shoves* MR PERRY *in.*

Well look who's here!! Let me, eh... Let me just...

He nods aggressively to MR PERRY *and leaves.*

MR PERRY. Well, Happy Thanksgiving, Marianne!

MARIANNE. Happy Thanksgiving, Mr Perry.

MR PERRY. How are you?

MARIANNE. Pretty much as well as I was when you saw me yesterday.

MR PERRY. I can worry about you, can't I?

MARIANNE. I guess. But you don't know me all that much.

MR PERRY. Would you believe me if I said I feel I do know you?

MARIANNE. How?

MR PERRY. I guess God's goodness shines down and it makes things happen. Things you couldn't dream of I guess.

ELIZABETH. I guess.

MR PERRY. Maybe my whole life has been leading me right here to give you and your child shelter. Who can say? (*Laughs pathetically.*) I mean, that makes about as much sense as anything else as far as I can make out!

MARIANNE. Maybe you're just a predator.

MR PERRY. A predator?

MARIANNE. Sure.

MR PERRY. I don't think so.

MARIANNE. Well how would you know?

MR PERRY. I think I'd know if I was a predator, Marianne.

MARIANNE. Maybe you wouldn't. Maybe you have to believe you're going round doing good deeds so as to enable you to go on the hunt. You know, on the prowl.

MR PERRY. I don't think so.

MARIANNE. No, huh? My pa didn't say nothing about all the trouble we had here?

MR PERRY. Trouble is everywhere. I know.

MARIANNE. I'm talking about troubles no one can explain.

MR PERRY. Explain what?

ELIZABETH *picks out a stark rendition of 'Ballad Of A Thin Man' on the piano.*

MARIANNE. That night. The night I... the night the wind came in my room. I woke up. All I knew then was... someone was there.

MR PERRY. A man came in your room?

MARIANNE. It was deeper than a man. Older than a man. When I pressed my face into his tunic and I breathed in, I could smell, like, ancient water. You know that smell like water under the ground? Like stone? And when I breathed in more and more it was like I was breathing through him. And I could see through him – into the ancient past. A figure in a boat, and someone was singing and I... That's how it happened.

MR PERRY. Marianne, however it happened, you got yourself in trouble. All your daddy wants is to look at our options here.

MARIANNE. You look like a weak man, Mr Perry. But you got some steel buried in there keeps you cutting in the woods.

Out in the kitchen a girl sings 'Girl From The North Country', other guests harmonizing.

MR PERRY. Hey! I don't need to come down here and be told I'm weak! You don't know what I been going through every day since your daddy came to me! What would you know about it? You haven't got a damned pot to piss in and you subject me to this? Let me tell you something. Your daddy can't take care a you. This house? It's gonna all be taken by the bank. Your daddy's too old to work on a farm or a factory – even if there was work. Bottle's got your brother. Who knows where your mama's gone? Where you gonna go? A black girl with a black baby? You want me to tell you? You're gonna be made to give that baby away and then you can whistle your way down to St Louis or somewhere, work as a maid. That's all you are. Now you and me both got a chance. My wife came and told me in a dream, Marianne. My wife!! You just get in under my roof, girl, and I won't never touch you, that's a promise.

The singing stops.

Nobody chooses to get old. Everybody fights it. But it kicks your ass. You can't win. You move slower and slower 'cause you can't go quicker! It hurts! Pain's got ya surrounded. In your back and your legs and your hands – in here in your gut. You wake in the night, there's no one there. Only the cold. And one way down. You remember a warm light and a smile from long ago. But doesn't help. It only hurts.

NICK *returns*.

NICK. So we doin'? Huh?

ELIZABETH. Oh he's just been showing everybody his Vienna sausage.

MR PERRY. Gimme a date and I'll write you a check.

NICK. How about Christmas Eve?

MR PERRY *nods*. NICK *shakes his hand*.

Stay for lunch.

NICK *spies* GENE.

So how you doing? You go down to that, eh...

GENE. Sure.

NICK. Well?

GENE. Yeah.

NICK. Yeah?

GENE. Yeah it's...

NICK. We're talking about the interview.

GENE. Yeah, I know.

NICK. And?

GENE. Yeah.

NICK. It's all good?

GENE. All good. He said the railroad's gonna lift all the boats round here. Bright guy like me, start in the office, working my way up...

NICK. That's right...

GENE. Said it was just what they wanted to see.

NICK. Didn't I tell you?

GENE. Yeah.

NICK. Huh?

GENE. Yeah.

NICK. You're a good boy.

GENE. I'm good boy.

> SCOTT *approaches* MARIANNE *to dance. She refuses him.*
> SCOTT *turns to see* ELIZABETH *waiting to dance with him.*
> *She curtsies, he bows, and they come together as 'Hurricane'*
> *begins.*

Hurricane

> Pistol shots ring out in the barroom night
> Enter Patty Valentine from the upper hall
> She sees the bartender in a pool of blood
> Cries out, 'My God, they killed them all!'
> Here comes the story of the Hurricane
> The man the authorities came to blame
> For somethin' that he never done
> Put in a prison cell, but one time he could-a been
> The champion of the world
>
> Three bodies lyin' there does Patty see
> And another man named Bello, movin' around
>   mysteriously
> 'I didn't do it,' he says, and he throws up his hands
> 'I was only robbin' the register, I hope you understand
> I saw them leavin',' he says, and he stops
> 'One of us had better call up the cops'
> And so Patty calls the cops
> And they arrive on the scene with their red lights flashin'
> In the hot New Jersey night

We segue into:

All Along The Watchtower

> All along the watchtower, princes kept the view
> All the women came and went, barefoot servants too
>
> Outside in the distance a wildcat did growl
> Two riders approaching, the wind began to howl

We segue back to 'Hurricane':

> When a cop pulled him over to the side of the road
> Just like the time before and the time before that
> In Paterson that's just the way things go
> If you're black you might as well not show up on the
>   street
> 'Less you wanna draw the heat

We segue to 'Idiot Wind':

Idiot Wind

MARIANNE.
> It was gravity which pulled us down and destiny which
>   broke us apart
> You tamed the lion in my cage but it just wasn't enough to
>   change my heart
> Now everything's a little upside down, as a matter of fact
>   the wheels have stopped
> What's good is bad, what's bad is good, you'll find out
>   when you reach the top
> You're on the bottom...
>
> Idiot wind...

MARIANNE *and* SCOTT.
> blowing every time you move your mouth
> Blowing down the backroads headin' south

MARIANNE.
> Idiot wind...

MARIANNE *and* SCOTT.
> blowing every time you move your teeth

MARIANNE.

> You're an idiot, babe
> It's a wonder that I still know how to breathe.

SCOTT.

> Idiot wind...

ALL.

> blowing through the flowers on your tomb
> Blowing through the curtains in your room

SCOTT.

> Idiot wind...

ALL.

> blowing every time you move your teeth

MARIANNE.

> I'm an idiot, babe...

ALL.

> It's a wonder that I still know how to breathe.

MRS BURKE. Happy Thanksgiving, Nick!

NICK. Happy Thanksgiving, Mrs Burke, Mr Scott.

SCOTT. Same to you, sir.

MRS BURKE. Where's Elias?

MR BURKE. We had a walk. He's sleeping. Well, look at all this! Happy Thanksgiving, Nick!

NICK. To you too – Marianne cooked the turkey, so...

MR BURKE. Marianne, you are a genius.

MARIANNE. I wouldn't say that. You can make yourself a sandwich – cranberry's all in the bowl.

MR BURKE. Holy shamoly.

NICK. We always do a sandwich. Then you don't have to do all that – you know – sitting at the same table, right?

MR BURKE. Yeah – everybody looking at each other! I get it. I'm the king of the sandwiches.

MRS NEILSEN. Here, let me make you one.

MR BURKE. I always liked you, Mrs Neilsen, you have a way about you. Doesn't she have a way about her?

MRS NEILSEN. What kind of a way?!

MR BURKE. A way! A way! Nick knows! Right? Am I right?

MRS BURKE. Ignore him, Mrs Neilsen. You think Elias wants a sandwich?

MR BURKE. Leave him, he's sleeping. (*To* MRS NEILSEN.) I dunno what it is – it's the confluence between your eyes and your eyebrows. Somehow they suggest a gateway to the eternal.

MRS NEILSEN. I'm just making you a sandwich!

MRS BURKE. What in God's name are you talking about?

MR BURKE. You look out, Joe, she's got them talons, once they get into you, you'll never get away.

SCOTT. I don't know about that, but she can dance.

MRS BURKE. You mind not talking about me like I'm not here?

SCOTT. I'm sorry, excuse me.

MR BURKE. It's only good things! We're only saying nice things! You look out. How many drinks has she had?

MRS BURKE. Not as many as you clearly. (*To* SCOTT.) I never felt arms like these.

SCOTT. Thank you, ma'am.

MRS BURKE. I mean it – you ever feel arms like that, Nick?

NICK. Not lately.

DR WALKER *comes to* MARIANNE.

DR WALKER. How are you, Marianne?

MARIANNE. Fine, thank you.

DR WALKER. You want to call by – next week?

MARIANNE. Sure.

DR WALKER. Unless you want to see someone else.

MARIANNE. No, that's fine.

MRS BURKE. Should I go get Elias? He's missing everything.

MR BURKE. Leave him alone.

NICK *comes through with fuel for the stove.*

NICK. Anyone been outside? Man, it's cold.

DR WALKER. Sure is.

MR BURKE. Mmm! You see the snow?

DR WALKER. Mm-hm.

NICK. That's how it starts. Those dry flakes like that? That's North Pole air. Frank, sit down!

MR BURKE. I'm good. I like standing. It's like swaying around on a ship.

MRS BURKE (*to* MR BURKE). You want to go easy?

MR BURKE (*calling to* NICK). A sick child gets inside you somehow, Nick.

NICK What's that?

MR BURKE (*calling to* NICK). I guess you can't help it. It's down there underneath everything.

MARLOWE *comes in.*

MARLOWE. Happy Thanksgiving. Hello, all. What about that wind! It's like a knife!

MR BURKE. Reverend. The very fellow. Happy Thanksgiving. Have a sandwich. I was just saying. A sick child.

MARLOWE (*instant sympathy*). Oh, but of course.

MR BURKE. I mean, one moment there you are, in your life, kind of a child yourself.

MRS BURKE. Oh where is he?

MRS BURKE *goes to find* ELIAS. MARLOWE *pulls away from* MR BURKE *as he rambles between the guests.*

MR BURKE. You have responsibilities, you have worries, sure, but it's mostly about yourself, your intended, your wife, the few dollars in your pocket, the normal things. And you think when that baby comes along how complete things will be. What no one tells you is – Jesus Christ – a child is hard work, brother!

For sure. Listen, I'm not saying I was there when it was hardest. I could escape to my office, find peace in my dreams and the hurly-burly and the fights and arguments which all men truly enjoy.

MRS BURKE *comes back through, looking for* ELIAS.

MRS BURKE. Where'd you say he was?

MR BURKE (*indicates vaguely*). He's… (*He blows a raspberry.*)

MRS BURKE. You need to lie down. (*To the others.*) I apologize.

MRS BURKE *pulls* MR BURKE *and puts him sitting beside* DR WALKER.

MR BURKE. She'll tell you. I tried – to put in the hours. It's… it's… I mean, it'll drive you crazy because a child is only learning. They wanna do the most mundane little thing over and over again – it's torture! If you're not in the mood, ha, ha, ha – (*A qualifying little laugh.*) Thinking to yourself, it'll get easier when he's older. But he never got any older! (*Laughs.*)

NICK. He's a good boy.

MR BURKE. Right! He just got bigger and bigger! The nights I stood on the landing outside his door, listening to the strange noises he made.

ELIZABETH *pulls* MR BURKE *up to dance.*

MR BURKE. Laura sitting inside in there with him. I was… afraid to go in. I could face down eighty men threatening to strike.

MR BURKE *is hurting* ELIZABETH *with his grip. He doesn't realize.* DR WALKER *extricates her.*

Righteous anger, lifting me up in a chariot of hatred, but a child's cries. A big grown child crying in the night, why, it rips the floor from underneath you. And then. In the crash. The money's gone. The business is gone. They say they're coming for your house! And there you are. You're naked. You have to just be a… a father. That's all you are. That's all that's left. But you're a father to this helpless… This creature. Full of strength and longings and drives he doesn't understand. You turn your back on him for one second and he gets out…

MRS BURKE *comes back.*

MRS BURKE. Francis…

MR BURKE. He gets out and you're frantically searching for him all up and down in the neighbors' yards…

MRS BURKE. Francis…

MR BURKE. If the unthinkable happens… if he's done something, to someone, it's… it's…

MRS BURKE. Francis…

MR BURKE. It's beyond a nightmare. 'Cause a nightmare ends.

MRS BURKE (*turning off the wireless*). Francis. Where's Elias?

MR BURKE. He's sleeping. I told you. We went for a walk is all. Went for one of our long ones. Down for a look at the water.

MRS BURKE. Where is he, Francis?

MR BURKE. I told you.

MRS BURKE. He's not here!

She goes out again. We hear her calling for ELIAS.

DR WALKER. Where is he, Frank?

MR BURKE. The water was like iron.

DR WALKER. Where is he?

MR BURKE. It was an accident. That's…

MRS BURKE *comes back*

MRS BURKE. Where is he?!

MR BURKE. It was an accident. I couldn't stop it.

NICK. Where is he, Frank?

MR BURKE. He's on the shore, Nick. He's asleep.

MRS BURKE....What?!

MARLOWE. Oh, Mrs Burke.

MR BURKE. Where's your God now, Reverend, huh?

MARLOWE. He's everywhere.

MR BURKE. That's right.

> MR BURKE *starts laughing*. ELIZABETH *joins in laughing with him*.

MRS BURKE. Are you all crazy? Are you all fucking crazy?

NICK. Frank. What happened?

MR BURKE. The water was like iron.

MRS BURKE. You fuckin'... You fuckin'... You didn't even...

> *She goes to* MR BURKE, *starts thumping him with her fists*.

You didn't even say nothin'. You never said a goddamn thing! You dirty bastard.

> ELIAS*'s ghost, free of pain, worry or limitations, enters*.

Duquesne Whistle

ELIAS.
> Listen to that Duquesne whistle blowin'
> Blowin' like it's gonna sweep my world away
> I'm gonna stop at Carbondale and keep on going
> That Duquesne train gonna ride me night and day
>
> You say I'm a gambler, you say I'm a pimp
> But I ain't neither one
>
> Listen to that Duquesne whistle blowin'
> Sound like it's on a final run
>
> Listen to that Duquesne whistle blowin'
> Blowin' like she never blowed before

Blue light blinkin', red light glowin'
Blowin' like she's at my chamber door

You smiling through the fence at me
Just like you always smiled before

Listen to that Duquesne whistle blowin'
Blowin' like she ain't gonna blow no more

Can't you hear that Duquesne whistle blowin'
Blowin' like the sky's gonna blow apart
You're the only thing alive that keeps me goin'
You're like a time bomb in my heart

I can hear a sweet voice gently calling
Must be the Mother of our Lord

Listen to that Duquesne whistle blowin'
Blowin' like my woman's on board

Señor (Tales Of Yankee Power)

KATE.
> Señor, señor…

ELIAS.
> can you tell me where we're headin'?
> Lincoln County Road or Armageddon?
> Seems like I been down this way before

KATE.
> Is there any truth in that, señor?
> There's a wicked wind still blowin' on that upper deck

ELIAS.
> There's an iron cross still hangin' down from around her neck

KATE.
> There's a marchin' band still playin' in that vacant lot

ELIAS.
> Where she held me in her arms one time and said, 'Forget
> me not'

KATE.
> Well, the last thing I remember before I stripped and kneeled

GENE.
>Was that trainload of fools bogged down in a magnetic field

KATE.
>A gypsy with a broken flag and a flashing ring

GENE.
>Said, 'Son, this ain't a dream no more, it's the real thing'

>…

KATE.
>Señor, señor, let's disconnect these cables
>Overturn these tables
>This place don't make sense to me no more
>Can you tell me what we're waiting for…?

We segue into:

Is Your Love In Vain?

MRS BURKE.
>Do you love me, or are you just extending goodwill?
>Do you need me half as much as you say, or are you just
>>feeling guilt?
>I've been burned before and I know the score
>So you won't hear me complain
>Are you willing to risk it all,
>Or is your love in vain?

MR BURKE.
>Are you so fast you cannot see that I must have solitude?
>When I am in the darkness, why do you intrude?

MR *and* MRS BURKE.
>Do you know my world, do you know my kind

MR BURKE.
>Or must I explain?

MR *and* MRS BURKE.
>Will you let me be myself

MR BURKE.
>Or is your love in vain?

MRS BURKE.

> Well I've been to the mountain and I've been in the wind
> I've been in and out of happiness
> I have dined with kings, I've been offered wings
> And I've never been too impressed

Segue into 'License To Kill':

ALL.

> I've been a noisemaker, spirit maker,
> Heartbreaker, backbreaker
> Left no stone unturned.
> May be an actor in a plot
> that might be all that you got
> 'Til your error you clearly learned.

Segue back to 'Is Your Love In Vain?':

MR BURKE.

> Can you cook and sew, make flowers grow
> Do you understand my pain?
> Are you willing to risk it all
> Or is your love in vain?

MRS BURKE.

> Can you cook and sew, make flowers grow
> Do you understand my pain?
> Are you willing to risk it all
> Or is your love in vain?

Evening. MARIANNE is alone. SCOTT comes in, packing his duffel bag, taking clothes that are drying near the stove. Outside a storm is blowing hard.

SCOTT. You given anymore thought to what I said?

MARIANNE doesn't answer.

You hear that storm? I gotta be on that boat leaves at ten o'clock. Else nobody'll be going anywhere. (*Pause.*) You gonna dignify me with an answer?

MARIANNE. What do you care where I go?

SCOTT. I don't know! Just feels like I gotta take you.

MARIANNE. And I just gotta go along?

SCOTT. I know you don't know me. I know it's crazy. But there's crazier things happened – in this house! – far as I can see.

MARIANNE. This is a bad time, Mr Scott.

SCOTT. It's always bad times!

MARIANNE. You know, they say some coloreds tried to rob a store in town last night.

SCOTT. I don't know a damn thing about that.

MARIANNE. No, huh?

SCOTT. I just told you. What am I? The only colored you ever seen?

MARIANNE. You're the only one I ever saw says he's no money, next day he's all for jumping on a boat – take along a woman he only just met.

SCOTT. I'm tryna do you a good turn, you wanna whip round, put this crap in my face?

MARIANNE *goes to the dresser, searching for something.*

Don't you walk away from me. Don't you walk away from me like that. If we're gonna go that road together, even for a short while, you best be able to look me in the eyes and know what I am. At least gimme that. I ain't got nothing else in it taking you on.

MARIANNE. No, huh? I ain't stupid.

SCOTT. I never said you was.

She shoves a newspaper at him.

MARIANNE. I can read a paper.

SCOTT. So what?

MARIANNE. I see two convicts escaped outta Peytonville a week ago. Who's the other one? That preacher? Goodbye, Mr Scott. Or whatever your name is.

SCOTT starts to go, but halts with his back to her. His head down.

SCOTT. Maybe I ain't never been no savior, but I ain't never killed no one either! And if I'm walking the streets right now when some judge says I gotta rot my life away in some rat hole, well maybe he's wrong! You think I'm the only nigger was in the joint serving somebody else's stretch? You look me in my eyes and if you don't believe me, that's alright. I'll go. But if you can see me... I'm saying, if you can see me...

MARIANNE *leaves.* SCOTT *picks up his things to go, but halts as* MARIANNE *comes back into the room. She approaches him and puts an arm on him to embrace him. He just looks at the floor, unable to meet her gaze.*

ELIZABETH *comes through in her nightdress, soaking wet.*

ELIZABETH. Fix me, Marianne. Fix me, will ya? I'm such a goddamn mess! What happened?

MARIANNE *starts to fix* ELIZABETH *up.*

MARIANNE. Mama, what if I told you, I'm going away.

SCOTT *leaves.*

ELIZABETH. You're not going away. You're not going away. You just got here.

MARIANNE. Mama... I'm going away.

ELIZABETH. Shhh. That's alright. That's alright. Just don't play with knives. You know the devil's only tryna be your friend 'cause you give him your blood.

MARLOWE *comes in carrying his suitcase and coat.*

MARLOWE. Evening...

ELIZABETH. Here he is, the word of the Lord. The walkin' word of Jesus Christ.

ELIZABETH *goes to him, looking for trouble.*

Hey! You ready for the parade, Padre?

MARLOWE. The parade?

MARIANNE *goes to get her coat.*

ELIZABETH. The parade – the parade. All the holy saints.
Parading up and down. The nuns showed us at Jesus camp last
summer – up at Camp Jesus. They had all the children doin' it.
(*Starts to demonstrate.*) Head up and shoulders back, parading
up and down – all night long. You go up, up, up, up. Wave and
turn round and you go down, up, up, up, up, wave and turn.
Then parade over this way and acknowledge the saints.

MARIANNE *comes back, buttoning her coat, to say goodbye,
but* ELIZABETH *brushes past her.* MARIANNE *leaves.*

And this way and acknowledge the damned, look at them all
there, God help them, and you parade over this way and
acknowledge all the babies who died unbaptized. And this
way, parading, parading, parading.

As she demonstrates, MARLOWE *goes to her box of dollars
under the chair. He takes her money, putting it in his trouser
pocket.*

Wait a minute. Now you just wait one goddamn minute.

She goes to him and tries to get her money back.

You give me that.

MARLOWE. Get your hands off me.

They struggle.

Take your hands off me!

ELIZABETH. You give me that!

MRS NEILSEN *comes in, carrying her dry cleaning in a
parcel.*

MRS NEILSEN. What are you doing?

MARLOWE. This woman is trying to rob me.

ELIZABETH. He took my dollars! You give 'em back.

They go at it again, struggling.

MARLOWE. I will call the police!

MRS NEILSEN *gets between them, she pulls* ELIZABETH
back.

I'm not gonna stay in this madhouse a moment longer.

ELIZABETH. Look! Look! He put my dollars in his pocket!

MRS NEILSEN. Where's her dollars?

MARLOWE. I have no idea.

ELIZABETH. They're in his pocket, Aggie.

MARLOWE. Oh, come on!

ELIZABETH (*going to his pocket and pointing*). You can see 'em through the material, look at 'em bulging in his pants.

MARLOWE. I've never been so insulted. Only this woman is so clearly unwell I'd fetch a lawman and have a case. But I am a gentleman and I believe in God's grace. Therefore I'll allow the matter lie and be about my way.

ELIZABETH *runs out*.

MRS NEILSEN. Did you take her dollars?

MARLOWE. Madam, I am warning you. Do not join this accusation. Good day.

MRS NEILSEN. Did you take her dollars, you panhandling son of a bitch?

MARLOWE (*menacing*). Madam…

MRS NEILSEN. You best give her something from the church.

MARLOWE. I have no church.

MRS NEILSEN. What a shocker. Give her some alms then. Ain't that what the Bible says?

MARLOWE. I am a poor man myself.

MRS NEILSEN. Show me your pockets.

MARLOWE. I beg your pardon?

MRS NEILSEN. Show me your pockets.

MARLOWE. What would that prove?

MRS NEILSEN. Humor me.

MARLOWE. Why don't you give her some alms? Ha? What you got in those pockets? I know you're coming into money, huh?

He crowds MRS NEILSEN, *walking against her.*

MRS NEILSEN. You stay off a me.

MARLOWE (*quietly*). You wanna get into this? You wanna get into 'What's in your pockets?' What's in *your* pockets, huh?

MARLOWE *pushes* MRS NEILSEN *against the furniture.*

ELIZABETH *comes in – a revolver in her hands.*

ELIZABETH. Hey, preacher.

MARLOWE. Jesus Christ!

ELIZABETH. That's right.

She shoots into the air, knocking plaster from the ceiling.

MARLOWE. I don't have your dollars!

ELIZABETH *cocks the revolver, aiming at his crotch.*

Alright, alright. I'm gonna give you some of my dollars, alright?

He pulls the dollars from his pocket and throws them on the ground.

ELIZABETH. Thank you! You see? Good manners will always trump a scoundrel.

MARLOWE. What about you? You wanna get paid?

He throws dollars at MRS NEILSEN.

GENE *comes in.*

This is a fucking madhouse.

ELIZABETH. Then get out, right?

MARLOWE. I'm getting out.

ELIZABETH. Well then go.

MARLOWE. I am.

ELIZABETH. Well go then.

MARLOWE. I'm going.

GENE. Mom.

NICK *comes in, breathless, wet and dirty from being up on the roof in the rain.*

NICK. What the hell is going on? (*To* MRS NEILSEN.) What happened?

MRS NEILSEN. Ask him.

MARLOWE. I have been accused and degraded, sir. Here in this very room.

NICK. We've all been degraded in this very room. Who was shooting?

MRS NEILSEN. It doesn't matter.

MARLOWE (*leaving*). With ye last prayers will ye seek ye repentance.

ELIZABETH. Ah fuck off!

MARLOWE (*as he goes*). With pleasure!

NICK (*to* GENE). See to your mother.

GENE *tries to sort* ELIZABETH *out. She knocks him away with a shout.*

GENE. You can't…

NICK. What?

GENE. She's gonna kill someone.

NICK. Mm. Water's pouring in up there. Goddamn pipes have burst. Only hope now is they'll freeze.

GENE. Right. You gonna go down the pier?

NICK. For what?

GENE. Marianne just told me that's where she's going. You have any opinion about that?

NICK (*shrugs*). That guy seems like a…

GENE. Like a what?

NICK (*wipes his nose while he tidies up*). He seems strong.

GENE. Well that's alright then. Too bad she didn't feel like saying goodbye I guess.

NICK. Well, that's...

GENE. What.

NICK. That's a pity.

GENE. That's a pity, huh?

NICK. I think so.

GENE. Yeah?

NICK. Yeah.

GENE. You don't give a damn.

NICK. I did my best.

GENE. You did your best.

NICK. What did you want me to do? What would you do? Kick her in the street?

GENE. Well she's in the street now! Why couldn't ya just let her stay here?

NICK. There is no here! I don't own a 'here'! I only ever borrowed it, Gene! You got a job and that's... it's gonna be okay.

MRS NEILSEN *takes her dry cleaning and heads out.*

GENE. I don't have a job.

NICK. But you had the letter.

GENE. I was too late. Job was gone.

NICK. And you just took that?!

GENE. Well what else could I do?

NICK. You coulda said something... Jesus Christ, you shoulda said something to me! What are you doing? Instead you lied to me about it?

GENE. I didn't want to embarrass you!

NICK. Embarrass me?

GENE. 'Cause you were all, 'This guy is my buddy. And she's my old girlfriend and this is all gonna be terrific.'

NICK. That's great, Gene.

GENE. What are you so worried about? My plans don't work out they don't work out, what do you care?

NICK. Because... because me and your mother...

GENE. What?

NICK. We're not gonna be here.

GENE. What... When?

NICK. I figured a way out.

GENE. What? What is it?

NICK. We're not gonna be here.

GENE. Where are you going?

NICK. We're going all the way.

GENE. All the way where?

NICK. All the way.

GENE. Don't joke like that, Dad.

NICK. It's no joke. Your mother will go first, and...

GENE. Don't joke like that.

NICK. It's alright. It's okay. It would have happened sometime, right? I been flailing around, Gene. I gotta stop.

GENE. Dad. Don't... don't do that. I'll get a job. I'll get one.

NICK. Yeah, get a job. A few dollars ain't gonna get us out of this one.

GENE. Give me a chance.

NICK. Whatcha gonna do? Suddenly write a masterpiece all of a sudden?

GENE. Maybe. Maybe I will.

Underscore of 'Lay Lady Lay' begins.

ELIZABETH. You've gotta go, Gene.

NICK *shakes his head.*

NICK. I'm sorry, son.

GENE. What?

NICK. Yeah.

GENE. Where am I gonna go?

NICK *puts his hand in his pocket.*

NICK. Go wherever you... This is twenty-two dollars... it's everything I got. Get yourself a drink.

The female ensemble sing 'Jokerman':

FEMALE ENSEMBLE.
    So swiftly the sun sets in the sky
    You rise up and say goodbye to no one
    Fools rush in where angels fear to tread
    Both of their futures, so full of dread, you don't show one
    Shedding off one more layer of skin
    Keeping one step ahead of the persecutor within

    Jokerman dance to the nightingale tune
    Bird fly high by the light of the moon
    Oh, oh, oh, Jokerman

DR WALKER *addresses us.* ELIZABETH *is playing 'Clair de Lune' on the piano.*

DR WALKER. Last time I saw Nick Laine was the morning of Friday November 30th 1934. Why'd I call by? Christ knows. He seemed good when I saw him. He seemed alright. That's the... That's something I've come to recognize. Once the decision is made. Hardest thing in life, right? Making up your mind?

Daylight. Time has passed. MRS NEILSEN *comes in to find* NICK, DR WALKER *and* MRS BURKE *in the dining room.* MRS BURKE *is making lists.*

MRS NEILSEN. Your taxi's outside.

MR BURKE (*entering with suitcases*). Thank you, Mrs Neilsen.

MRS BURKE. Oh Mrs Neilsen, we are going to miss you.

MRS NEILSEN (*helping* MRS BURKE *into her coat*). I will miss you. I'm only sorry I won't be able to be with you for the ceremony.

MRS BURKE. We could never ask you to come all the way back east with us! We'd never expect it.

MRS NEILSEN. Is there anything I can do?

MRS BURKE. Oh no. When we get home it's… it's only going to be small – of necessity – but we'll… It's a pretty cemetery, Mrs Neilsen, it's… (*She fights back tears.*) Good and evil – it's all beyond them, isn't it?

MRS NEILSEN. Oh entirely.

MR BURKE. Well, I was talking to a friend of the coroner's assistant last night and he said, that slipway is notorious where he… You turn round, someone is gone, and the current just…

DR WALKER. It's not the first time.

MRS BURKE. They really need to…

MR BURKE. It's crazy!

MRS NEILSEN. Yes, it's terrible.

MR BURKE. You've been a good friend to us, Mrs Neilsen. You make sure and write. We should stay in touch.

MRS NEILSEN. Absolutely. Let me walk you out.

DR WALKER *is alone with* NICK *and* ELIZABETH.

NICK. You okay, Doc? You want some coffee?

DR WALKER. No, I better go.

DR WALKER *pauses at the door*.

I've always admired you, Nick.

MRS NEILSEN *comes in*.

NICK. Are you fucking crazy?

DR WALKER (*as he goes*). No, I... You just keep on that road, alright?

NICK (*to* MRS NEILSEN). What time is your bus?

MRS NEILSEN. Eleven.

NICK. You want something to eat?

MRS NEILSEN *shakes her head.*

You look very pretty.

MRS NEILSEN. I got a child inside me, Nick.

NICK. What? How did that happen?

MRS NEILSEN. The way it usually happens.

NICK. I thought you was too old.

MRS NEILSEN. Why thank you. I guess not.

NICK. Jesus Christ. You can't go now.

MRS NEILSEN. Why not? (*She kisses* ELIZABETH.) Goodbye, Elizabeth.

ELIZABETH (*gripping* MRS NEILSEN*'s hands*). You're too good for him, Mrs Neilsen.

MRS NEILSEN *silently goes out.*

Well, mister. You done it. You got 'em all out. I don't know how. But you did it.

I know. You start off — it's a love story. You wait outside the drug store where you said you'd meet her, searchin' in the eyes of everyone passing by. You can't believe it when she steps out of the crowd. Her face, perhaps plain to everybody else, well it uncloaks its beauty just for you. And you know you're gone. You're her hostage. And she takes you down into a world of plans and dreams you could never have sustained on your own.

And then one day in the midst of the exhilaration and the worry and the children and the fighting and the whole damn shebang, you look up and you see her again and you may as well be looking at a baby giraffe in the zoo.

She's alive and she sees you but her world is not your world. You don't want to live in her world and she doesn't want you there anyhow. But you know you're too weak on your own. The children look to you. 'What are you looking at me for?' you say. And they hate you and you're glad they hate you. 'Cause they stop coming to you.

And then one day she turns round and says, 'I don't love you anymore either' and you think, 'What the fuck does that have to do with anything?!' Except you know she's just knocked you out cold.

Intro to 'Forever Young' begins.

And you realize 'Oh shit, I'm really on my own here now. Okay, okay, that's alright. I can drink myself to death in some room somewhere – it's alright.'

Until she loses her mind. And then you have her forever. You have her forever.

ELIZABETH *sings.*

Forever Young

ELIZABETH.
>May God bless and keep you always
>May your wishes all come true
>May you always do for others
>And let others do for you
>May you build a ladder to the stars
>And climb on every rung
>May you stay forever young
>Forever young, forever young
>May you stay forever young
>
>May you grow up to be righteous
>May you grow up to be true
>May you always know the truth
>And see the lights surrounding you
>May you always be courageous
>Stand upright and be strong
>May you stay forever young

Forever young, forever young
May you stay forever young

DR WALKER *is before us. The full company sings
underscore throughout this speech until the final blackout.*

DR WALKER. When the bank foreclosed, Nick headed south,
took Elizabeth with him, took care of her best he could. Made
it down as far at Sioux City 'til Bronchitis got her in a
flophouse down there. They took her into a home for women
on the banks of the Missouri. Nick stayed nearby in a hostel
for men. Came down to see her every day. He was with her
the morning she passed. Held her hand at the end, I heard.
I don't know where he went after that. Word was he kept on
heading south, maybe down towards Oklahoma, but nobody
really knew.

We see NICK *and* ELIZABETH *having dinner – happy and
healthy.* GENE *joins them.*

Old Mr Perry gave Gene a place to stay and a job working in
his store. He tried his hand at reporting for a local paper then
took the plunge and moved down to New York City. He met a
girl there, it didn't work out. When the war came he enlisted
in the marines and saw action in Italy and then at Okinawa
where he stood on a mine and was declared missing in action
June of '45.

MARIANNE *comes and sits. The family is happy together.*

But I had already left this world eleven years earlier, on
Christmas Eve 1934. Set it all up. It was just like stepping
through a glass wall. I could still see everything. Saw the time
come and go. Saw Marianne and her Joseph come by the
following winter. And damn if she didn't have a baby in her
arms! Yes, she had a baby. They were well dressed in warm
coats. Came up and stood outside the old inn with that baby
in their arms. They looked up at the windows a while, then
I watched them walk away.

I looked out on the water. Then I closed my eyes.

Fade to black.

Coda:

Pressing On

MRS NEILSEN.

> Well I'm pressing on
> Yes I'm pressing on
> Well I'm pressing on
> To the higher calling of my lord
>
> Well I'm pressing on
> Well I'm pressing on
> To the higher calling of my Lord
>
> Many try to stop me, shake me up in my mind
> Say 'Prove to me that he is Lord, Show me a sign'
> What kind of sign they need when it all comes from within
> When what's lost has been found what's to come has
>   already been?
>
> I just keep pressing on
> On and on and on and on
> Pressing on
> I keep pressing on
> To the higher calling of my Lord
>
> Pressing on
> On and on and on and on
> I keep pressing on
> I keep pressing on
> To the higher calling of my Lord

ALL.

> And on and on and on and on.

> *Black.*

Afterword

In the foreword to the first edition of this play I wrote, 'I write this on the eve of moving from the rehearsal room to the theatre. Whatever happens next I have no idea.' Now, five years later, I can fill in something of what happened next.

When I wrote that foreword I was staying in a little house on Copperfield Street in South-east London. Each day I travelled over to Bermondsey where we rehearsed in a disused school hall.

I was very happy and inspired during this time. As a playwright, writing a play, you spend a lot of time alone. But as a director you finally get to work with a whole crowd of people. Whether you are auditioning actors, planning scenes with designers or, in the case of *Girl from the North Country*, working with musicians, you are never alone.

During early workshops for the show, the Old Vic management had introduced me to our music arranger, Simon Hale, and we immediately hit it off. There was a spontaneous joy in belting out Bob Dylan songs and figuring out ways to perform them that made us smile a lot. Alongside our choreographer, Lucy Hind, our scenic and costume designer, Rae Smith, sound designer, Simon Baker, and lighting designer, Mark Henderson, we set out with our cast to discover exactly what the show could be.

In the early days of rehearsal, I would play guitar as part of our little band. This meant I could bring songs into the rehearsal room each day, teach them to the cast, and we could decide very quickly if they might work or not.

An instructive moment occurred early on when Sheila Atim, playing Marianne, spoke about the song 'Tight Connection To My Heart (Has Anyone Seen My Love)'. She said, 'I was listening to Bob Dylan singing different versions, and I still can't work out the melody.' Given that Bob has his own unique way of expressing his songs – sometimes suggesting the melody rather than rigidly sticking to it, we realised that the only way to proceed was for Sheila to *decide* on a melody.

This way of working became key to our process. Just as Bob Dylan often finds new ways to perform his songs in concert, so our cast would have to find a way of singing that made sense to them. Bob's songs really allowed this freedom – which found its way into our storytelling.

The unconscious dream world of our characters was expressed beautifully by Bob's artistry – because his songs express everybody's dream world. So we could allow the songs to carry a lot of the emotional burden of the story.

As a playwright who has written many plays without music I am constantly longing for that mysterious space between the words; where the actors express something more telepathically powerful than anything I can write on a page – where the subtext soars above the lines. And music can vastly accelerate that process. I felt like I had been climbing at high altitudes in thin air, and now someone had pulled out a huge pressurised tank and said, 'Hey, you want some of this oxygen? It's called music!'

The night of the first preview I ate in a café near my digs and arrived to The Old Vic half an hour before the show. The audience was already assembling. It is always a shock when you have been rehearsing in your private world without an audience and the inevitable day comes when you must present the work in public. And you realise you have only been half alive.

The first act went without incident. The audience were clearly with it and enjoying it. But, taking no chances, as soon as the lights came up for the interval, I ran backstage in order to avoid hearing any negative comments. I found refuge in the kitchen at the top of the building. There was no one there. I put on the kettle for a cup of tea I didn't want, but I couldn't quite escape the theatre because the tannoy was on so that actors backstage can always hear the show and won't miss their cue.

The sound through the speaker from the auditorium was like an energised hive of bees – the excited buzz of conversation. This told me two encouraging things – firstly, the audience hadn't left the building, and secondly, they wanted to discuss what they had seen. So I felt we had a chance.

Given that we had developed the production organically through the rehearsal process, I could see the storytelling confidence growing as the second act progressed. If the first act plays more like straight drama interspersed with songs, the second half seems bolder than first, taking more risks – in places even aspiring to the operatic. The songs strain at the bounds of the drama and play tricks with our sense of time.

There is a peculiar silence in the theatre when a show is working. You can feel the stillness and concentration. The laughs are unified and the sense of listening is almost corporeal. Towards the end of the show I feared the audience might become restless during Shirley Henderson's final speech as Elizabeth, but no, they remained silent and focused all the way through her beautiful rendition of 'Forever Young' and Ron Cook's closing passage as Dr Walker.

The lights came down and a moment of silence fell through the darkness before the applause began. As soon as the lights came up for the curtain call, people rose to their feet in staggered clumps, as though dazed, and within moments it seemed as though everyone was on their feet and cheering.

Going on past experience, a response like that to a first preview is very rare – and it usually means you have a hit on your hands. And so it proved. But what surprised me most was how busy the show has kept me subsequently with so many new productions, reinventing and rediscovering the show to suit the talents of new cast members each time.

As I write this, the show is running in my home town of Dublin. It's finally made it here, and thankfully audiences have taken it to their heart in a way I could only have hoped for. And just like Bob Dylan's incredible journey through music, what I have continued to learn is that you can't predict anything in art. If you're lucky enough to be there when it happens, and even luckier to make your living doing it, you couldn't possibly wish for more.

Conor McPherson
Dublin, July 2022

Acknowledgements

All words and music by Bob Dylan, unless otherwise indicated.

'Sign On The Window'
Copyright © 1970 by Big Sky Music; renewed 1998 by Big Sky Music. All rights reserved. International copyright secured. Reprinted by permission.

'Went To See The Gypsy'
Copyright © 1970 by Big Sky Music; renewed 1998 by Big Sky Music. All rights reserved. International copyright secured. Reprinted by permission.

'Tight Connection To My Heart (Has Anyone Seen My Love)'
Copyright © 1985 by Special Rider Music. All rights reserved. International copyright secured. Reprinted by permission.

'Slow Train'
Copyright © 1979 by Special Rider Music. All rights reserved. International copyright secured. Reprinted by permission.

'License To Kill'
Copyright © 1983 by Special Rider Music. All rights reserved. International copyright secured. Reprinted by permission.

'I Want You'
Copyright © 1966 by Dwarf Music; renewed 1994 by Dwarf Music. All rights reserved. International copyright secured. Reprinted by permission.

'Like A Rolling Stone'
Copyright © 1965 by Warner Bros. Inc.; renewed 1993 by Special Rider Music. All rights reserved. International copyright secured. Reprinted by permission.

'Make You Feel My Love'
Copyright © 1997 by Special Rider Music. All rights reserved. International copyright secured. Reprinted by permission.

www.nickhernbooks.co.uk

facebook.com/nickhernbooks

twitter.com/nickhernbooks